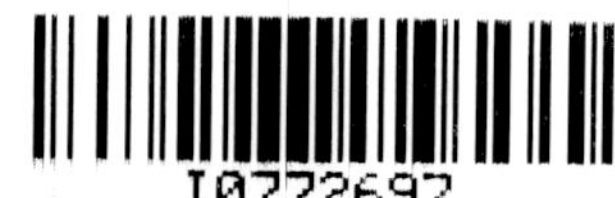

MAGICAL
FAIRIES & MERMAIDS
COLORING BOOK

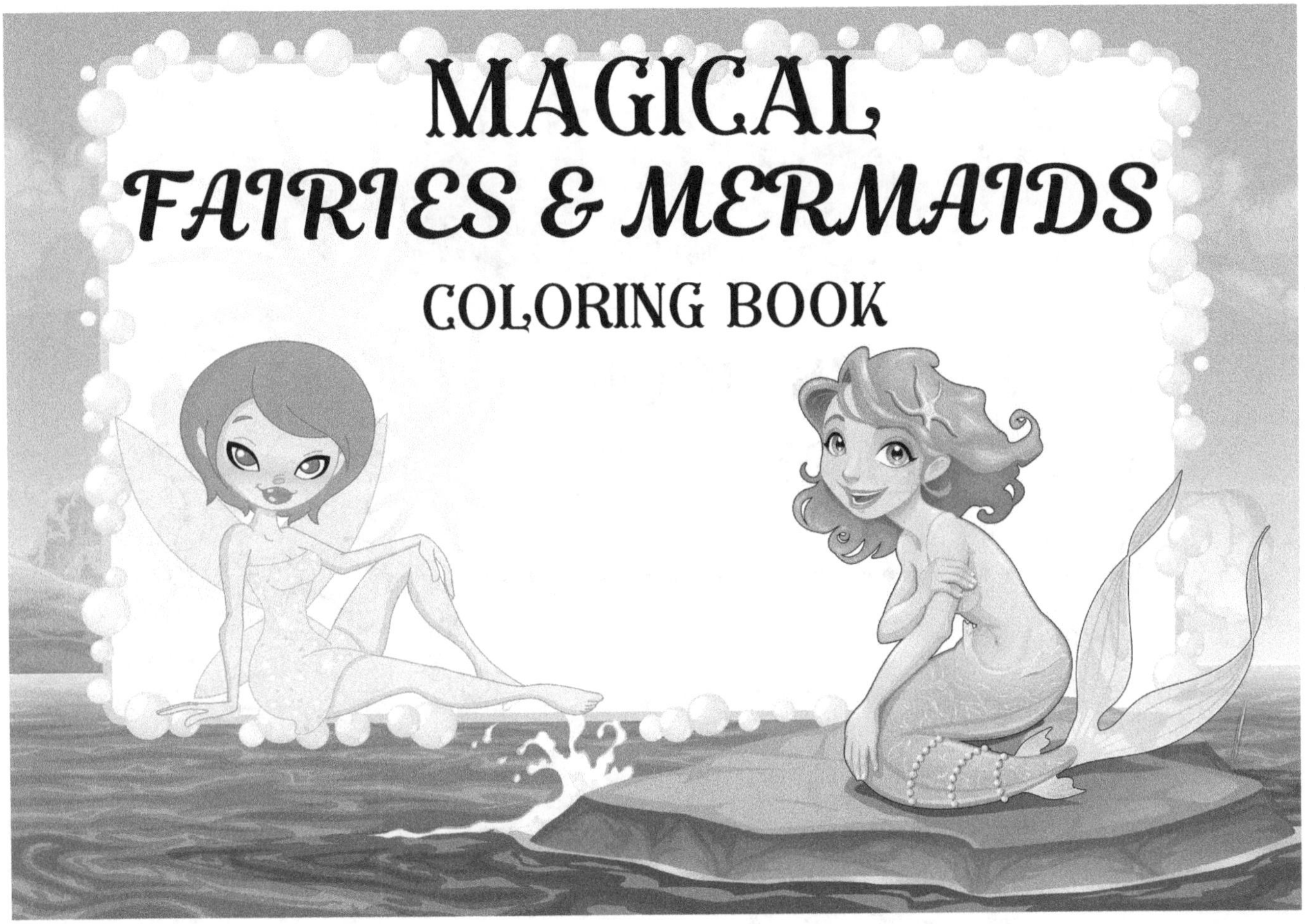

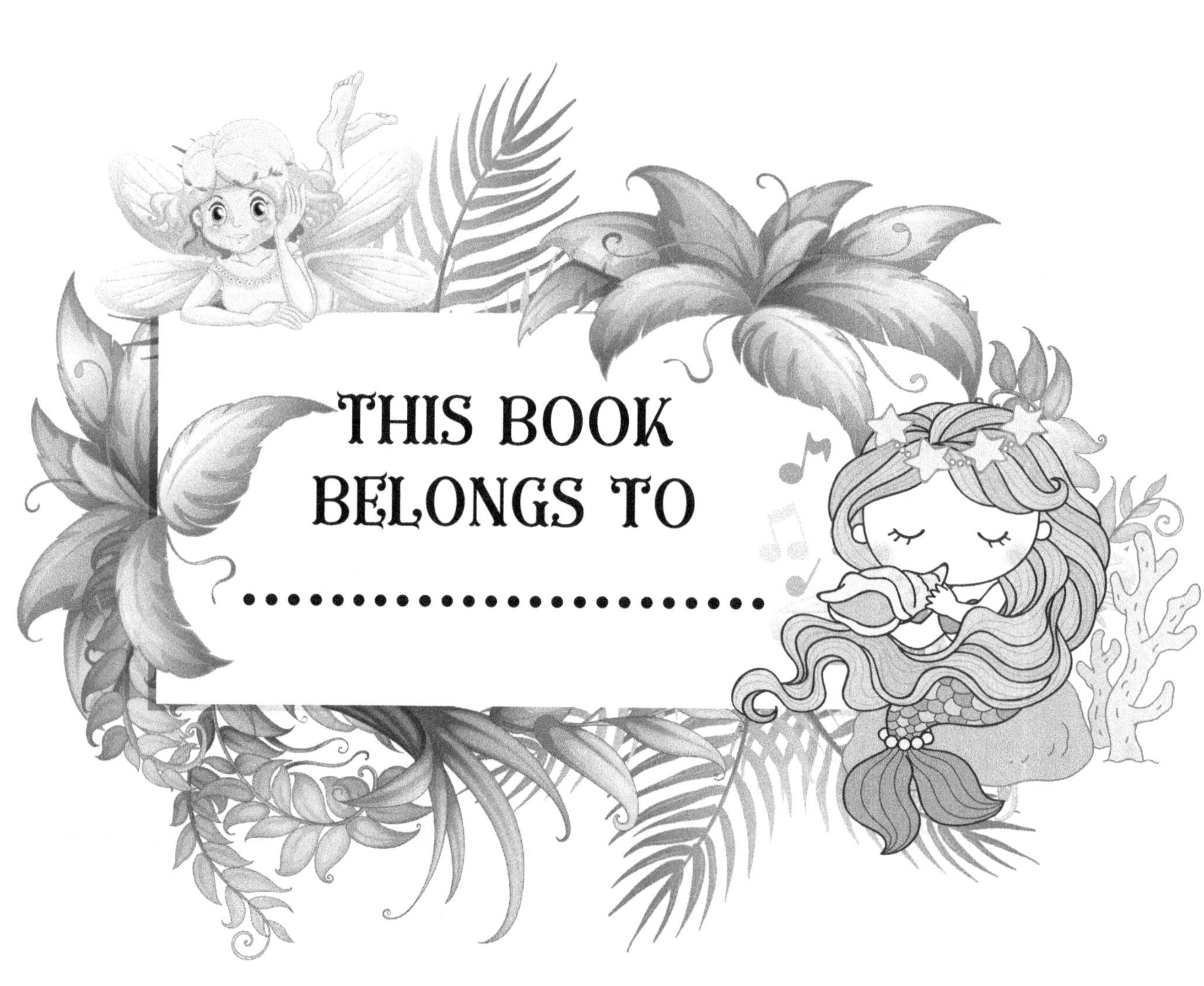
THIS BOOK
BELONGS TO
....

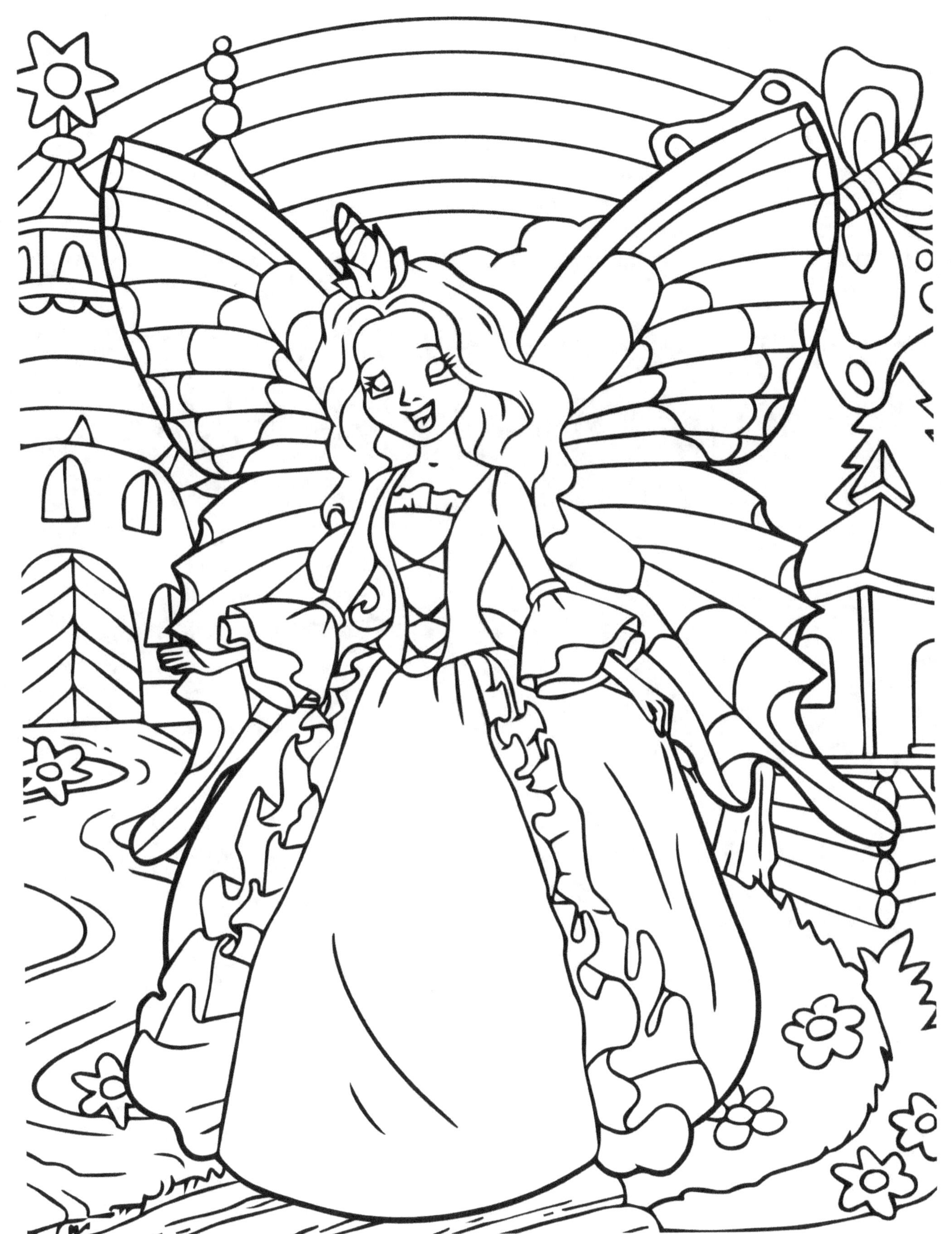

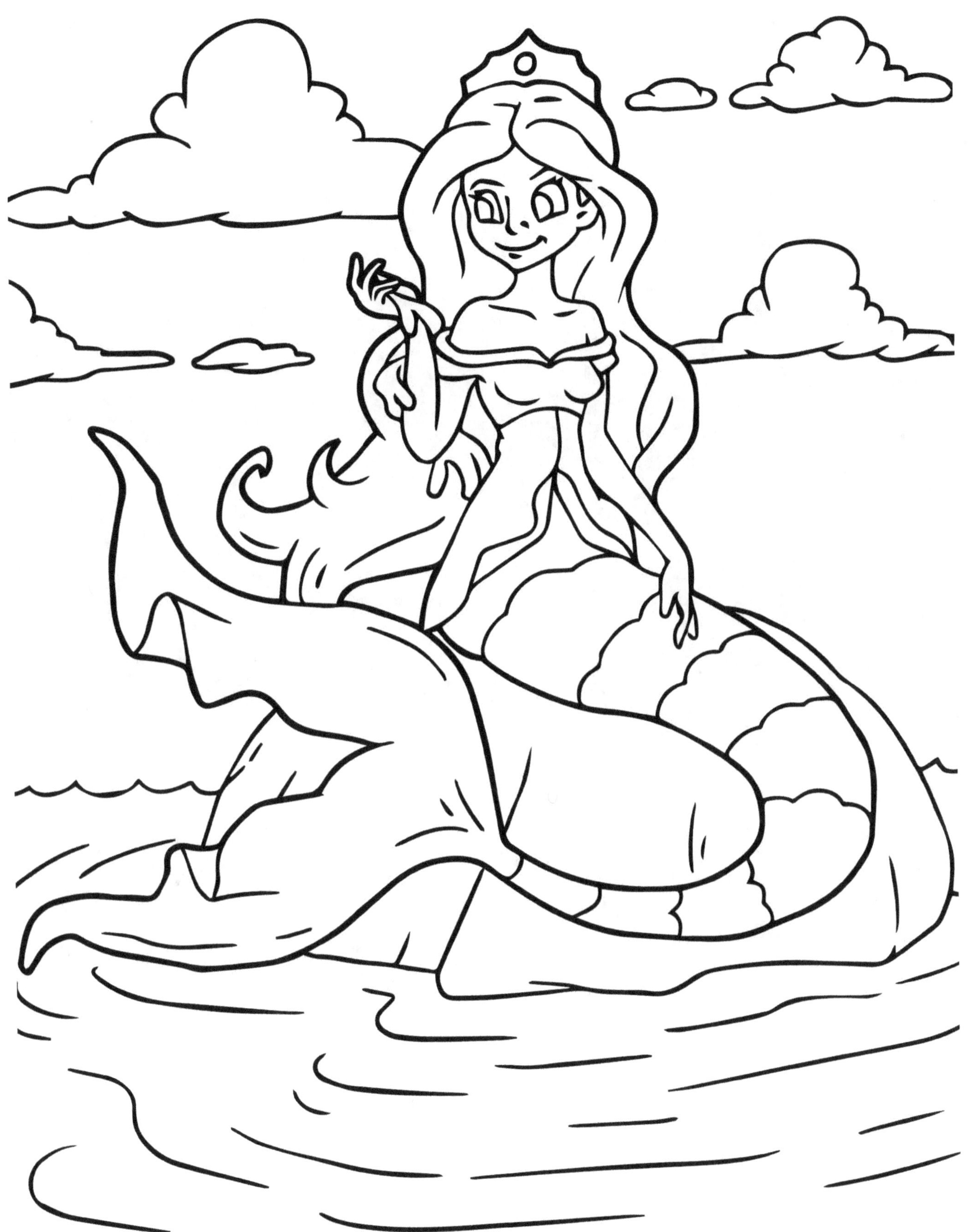

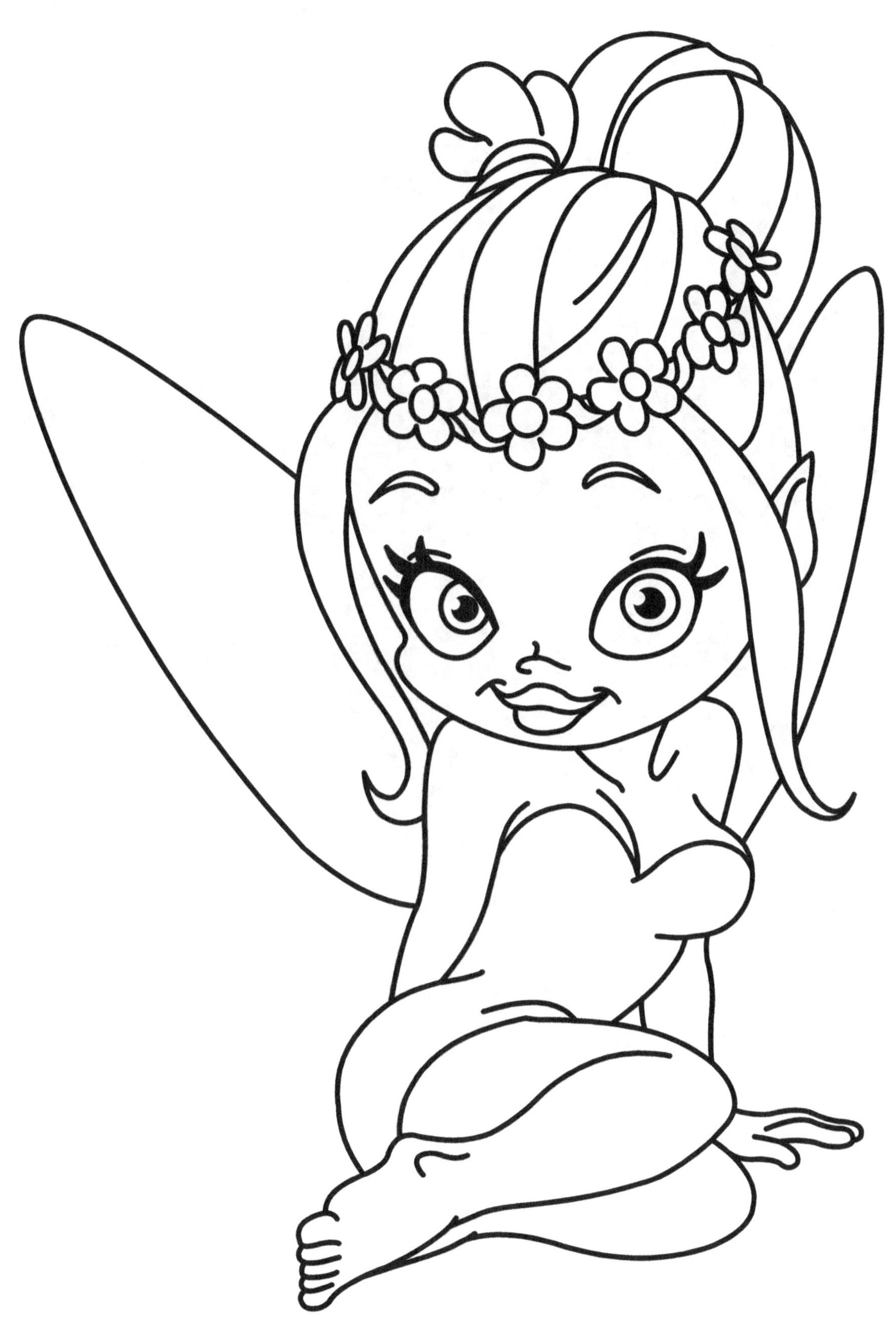

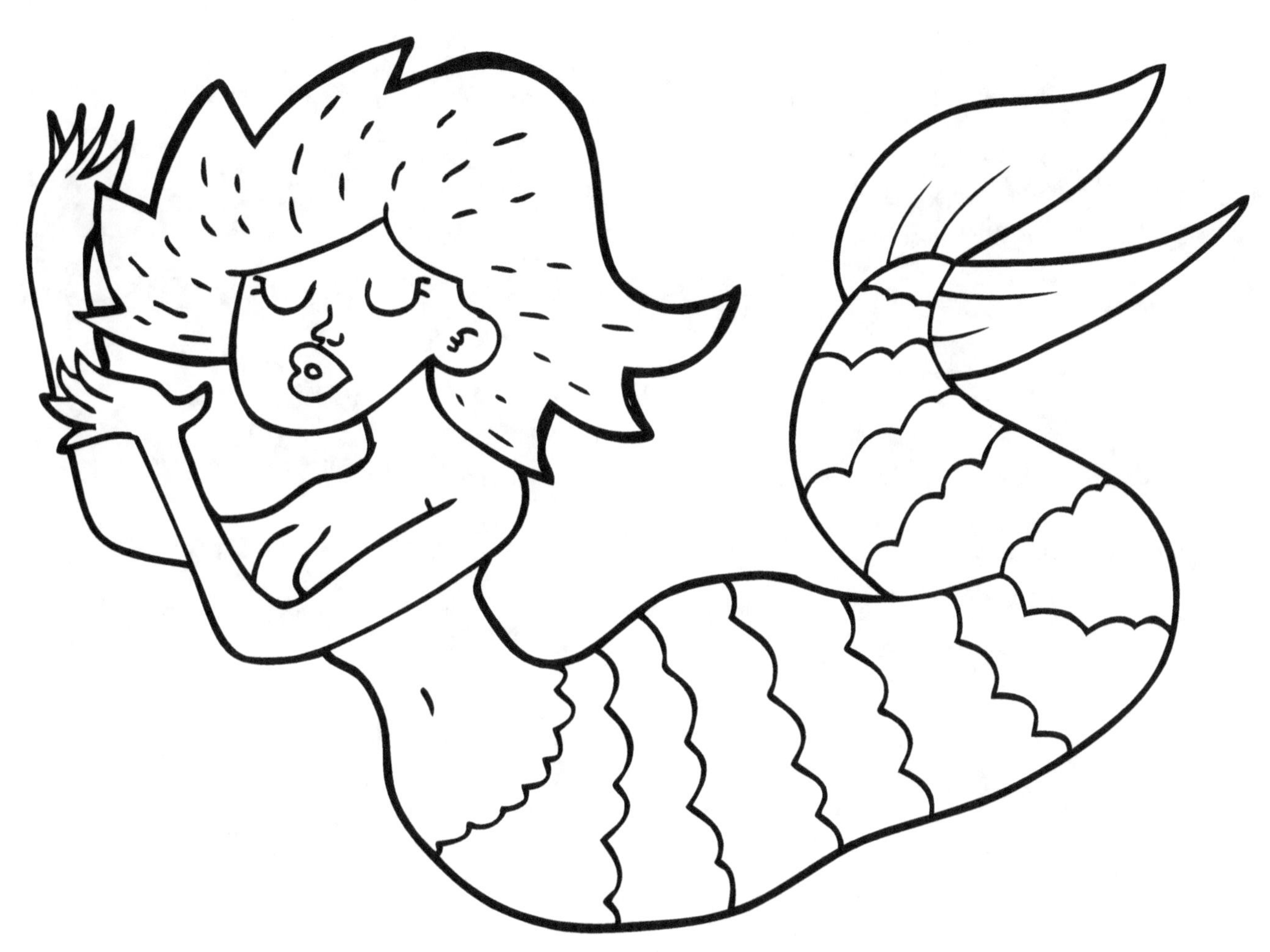

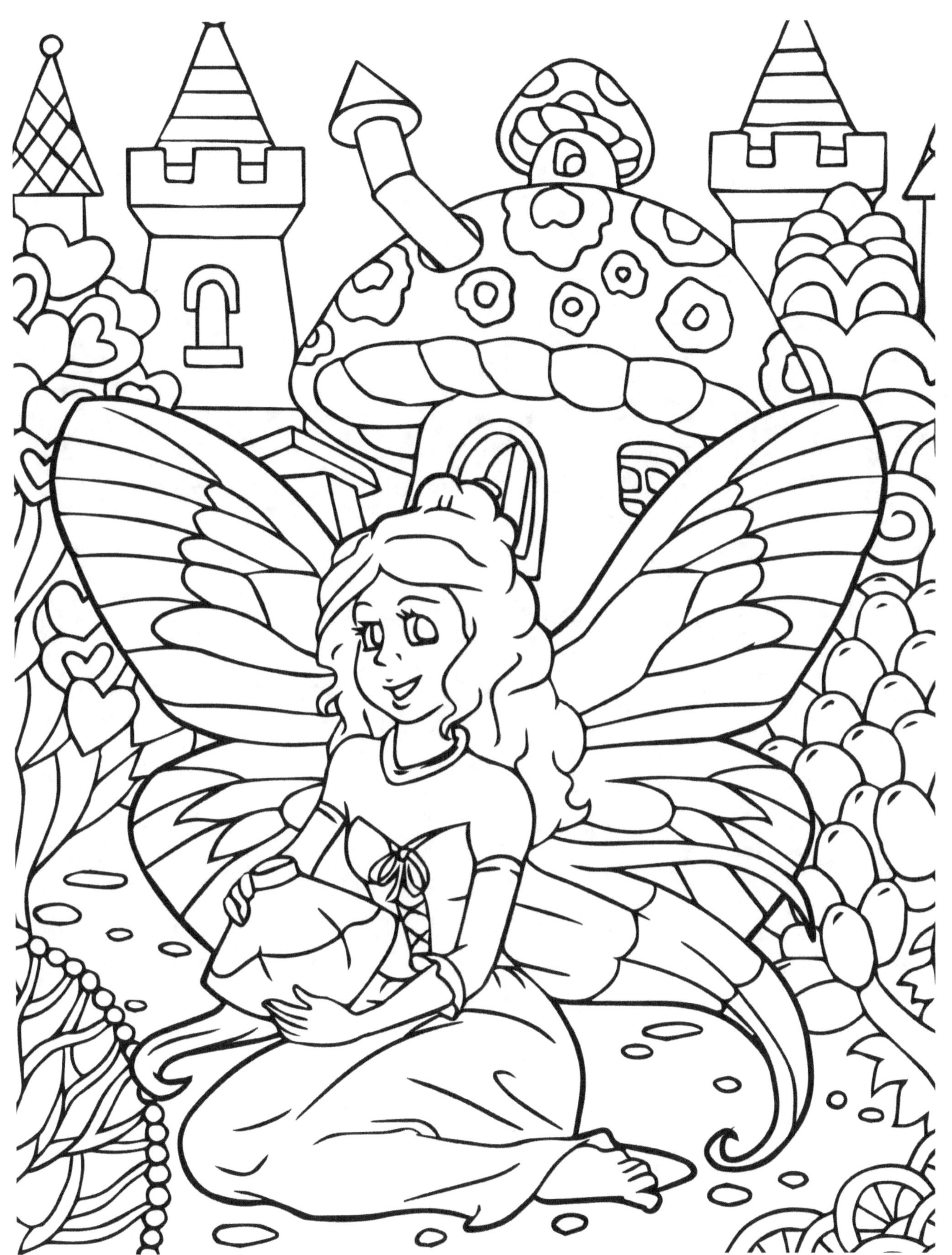

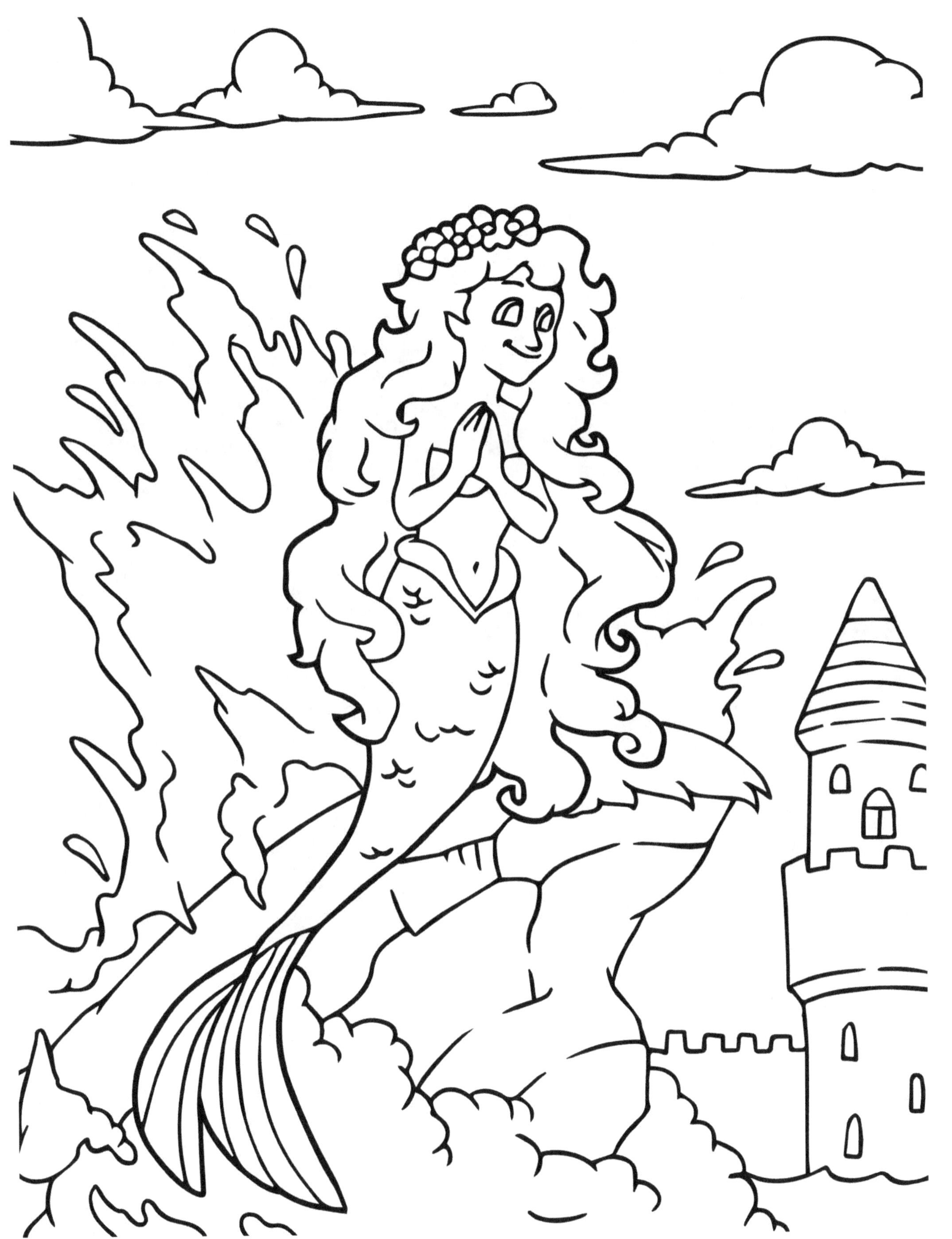

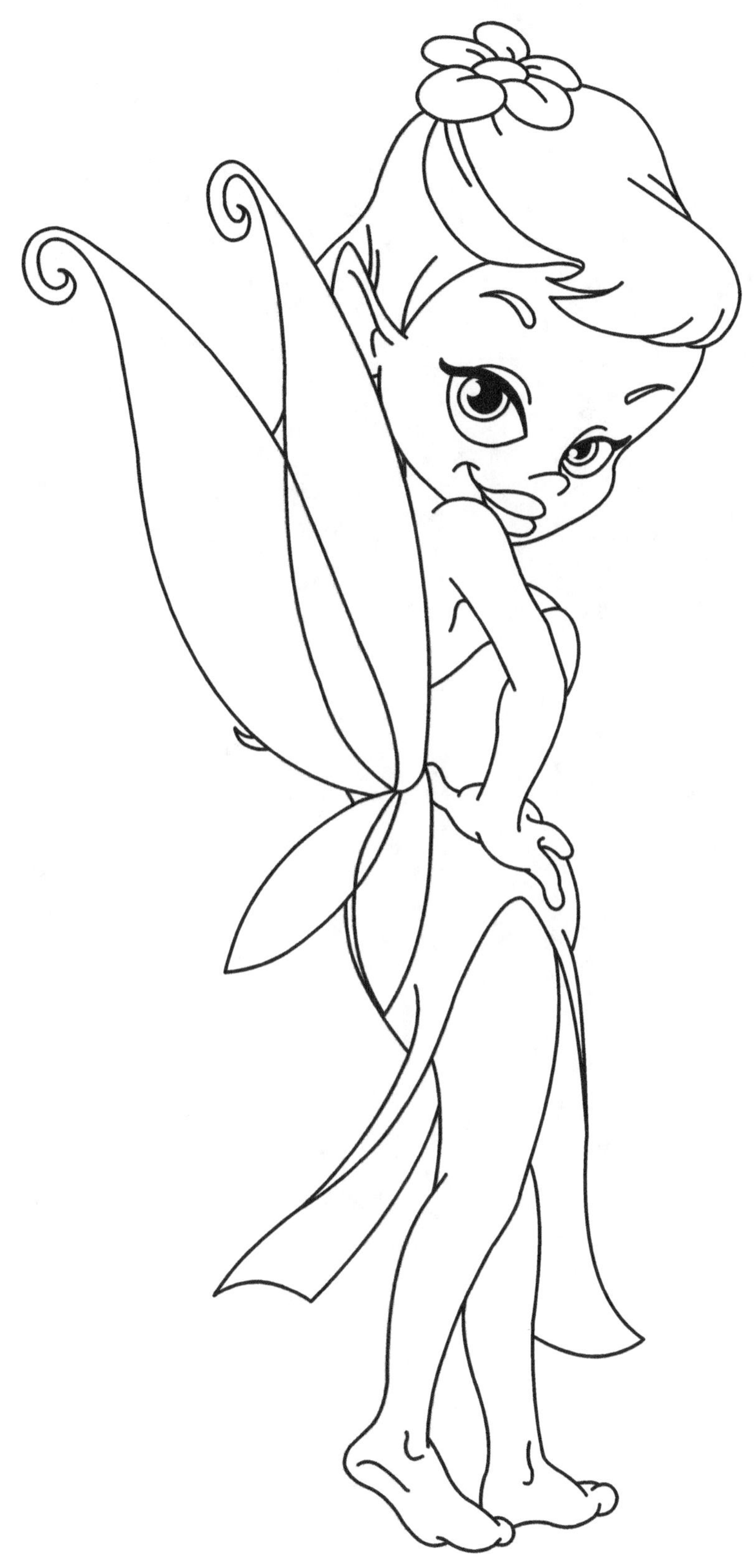

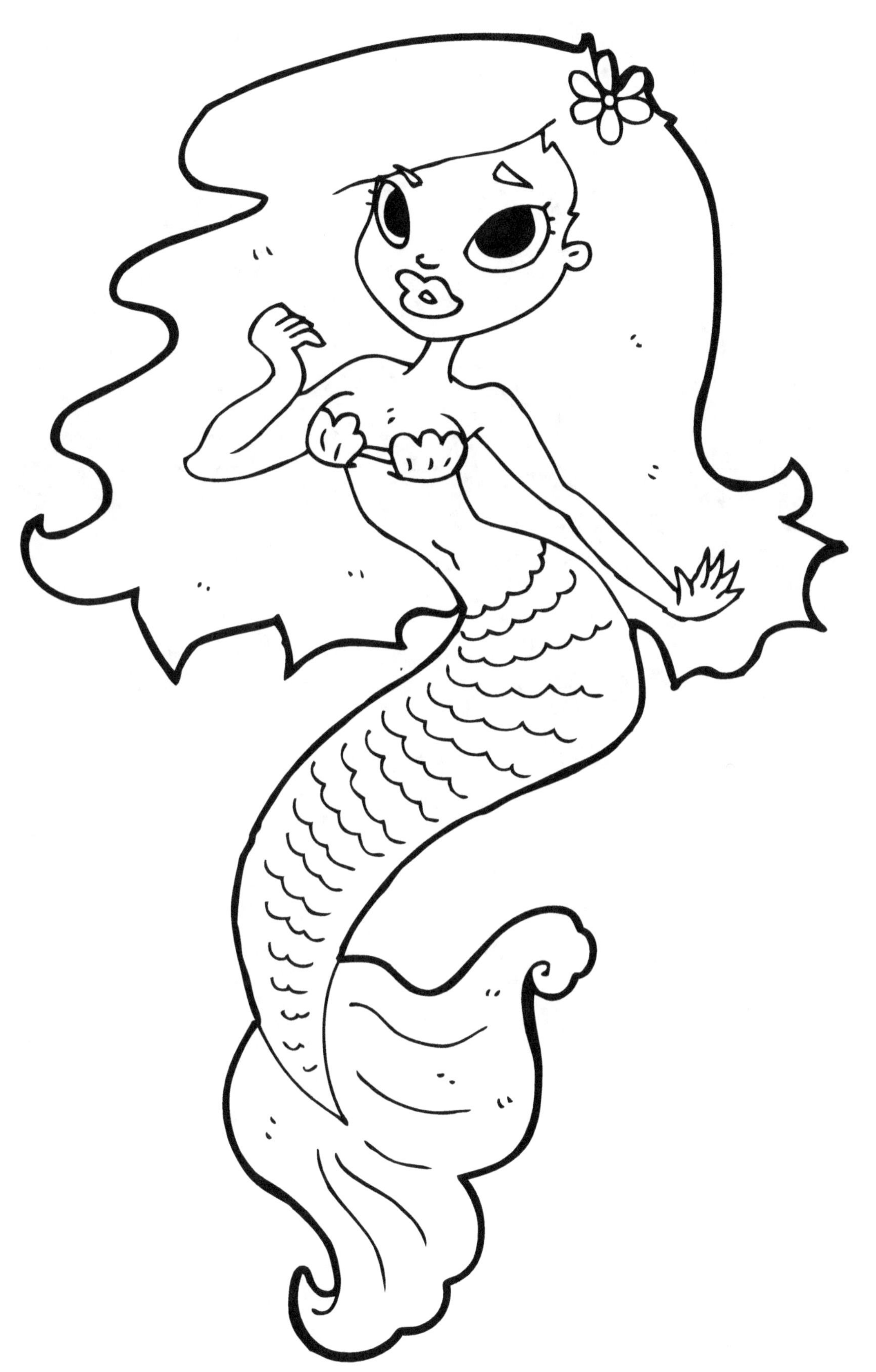

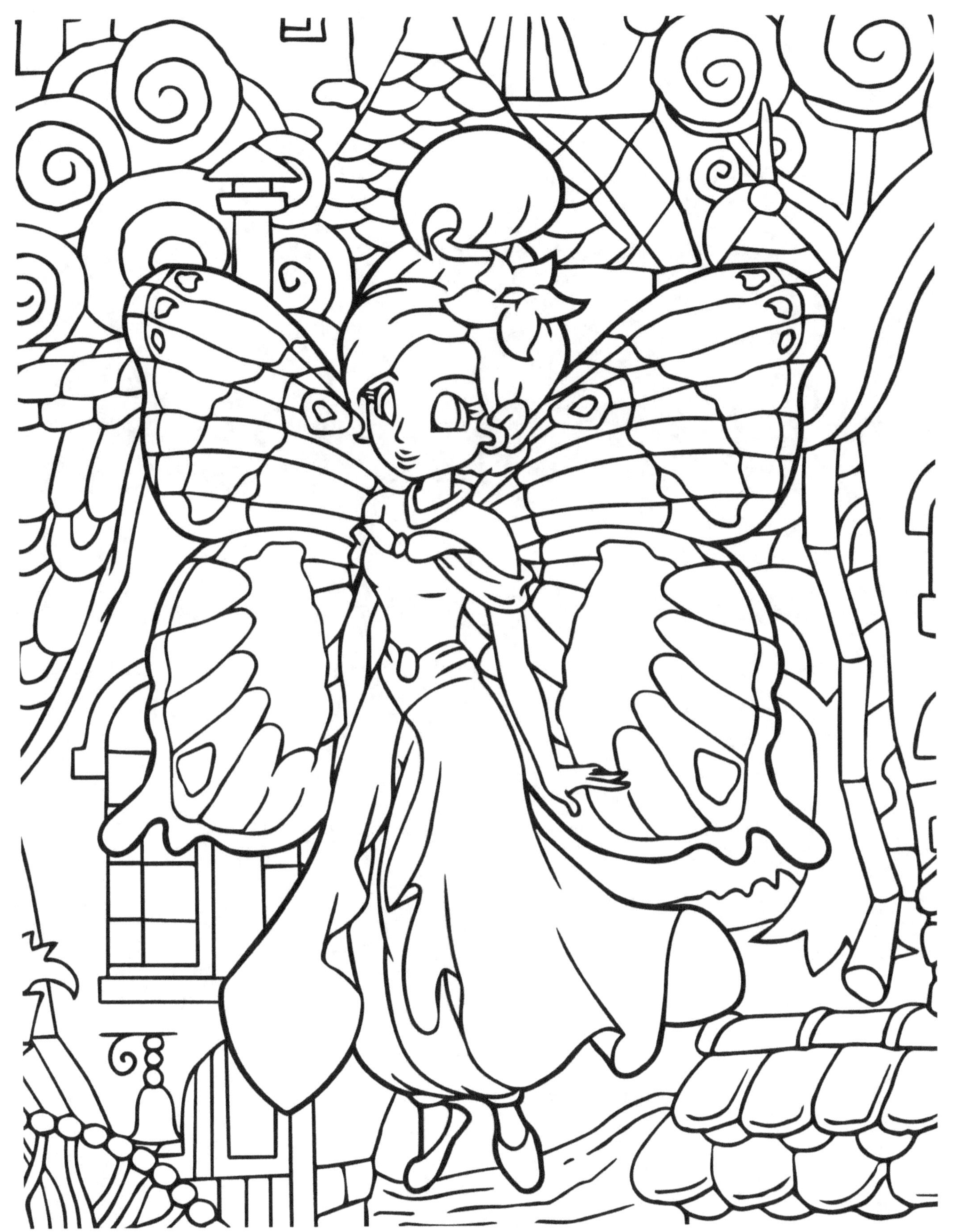

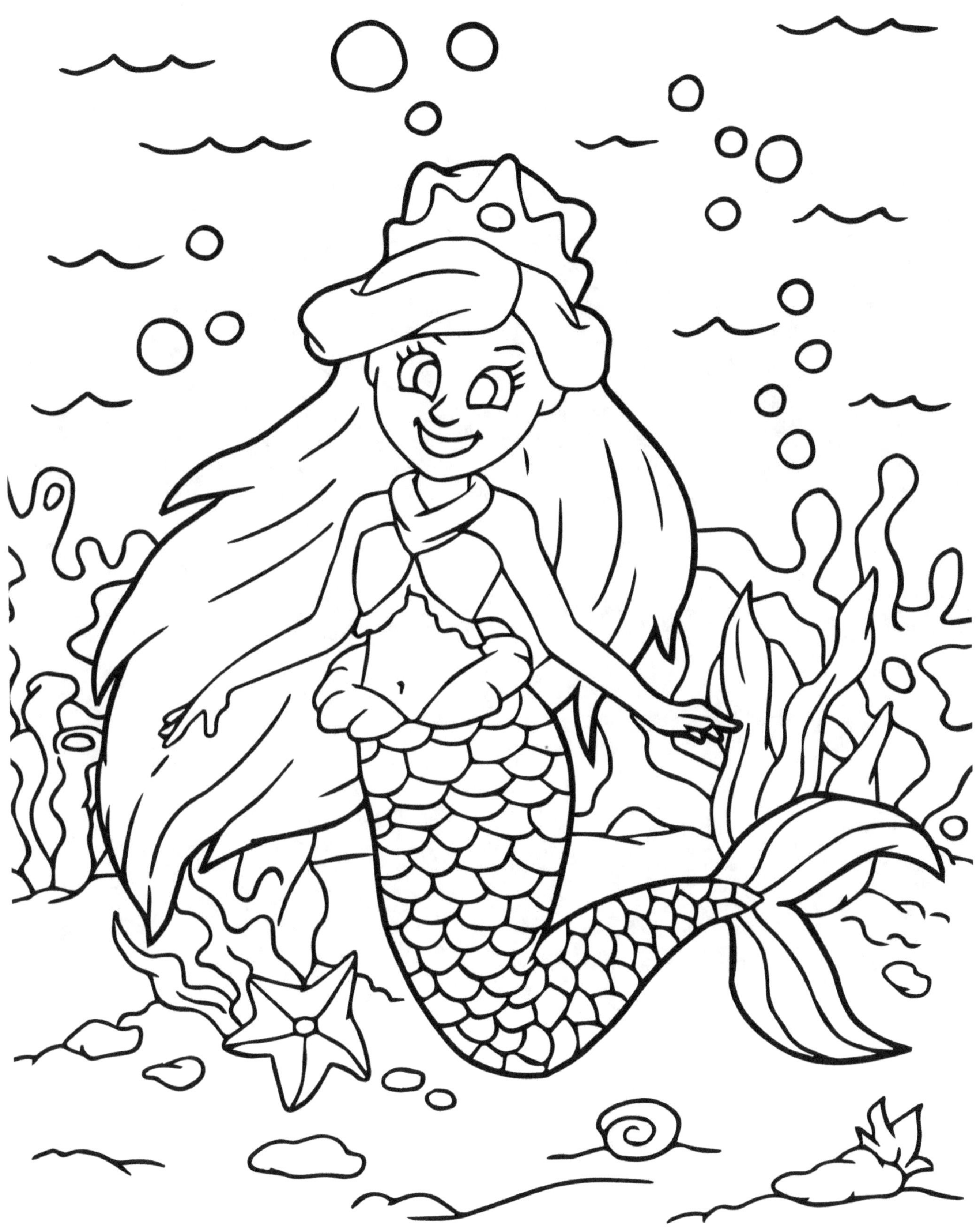

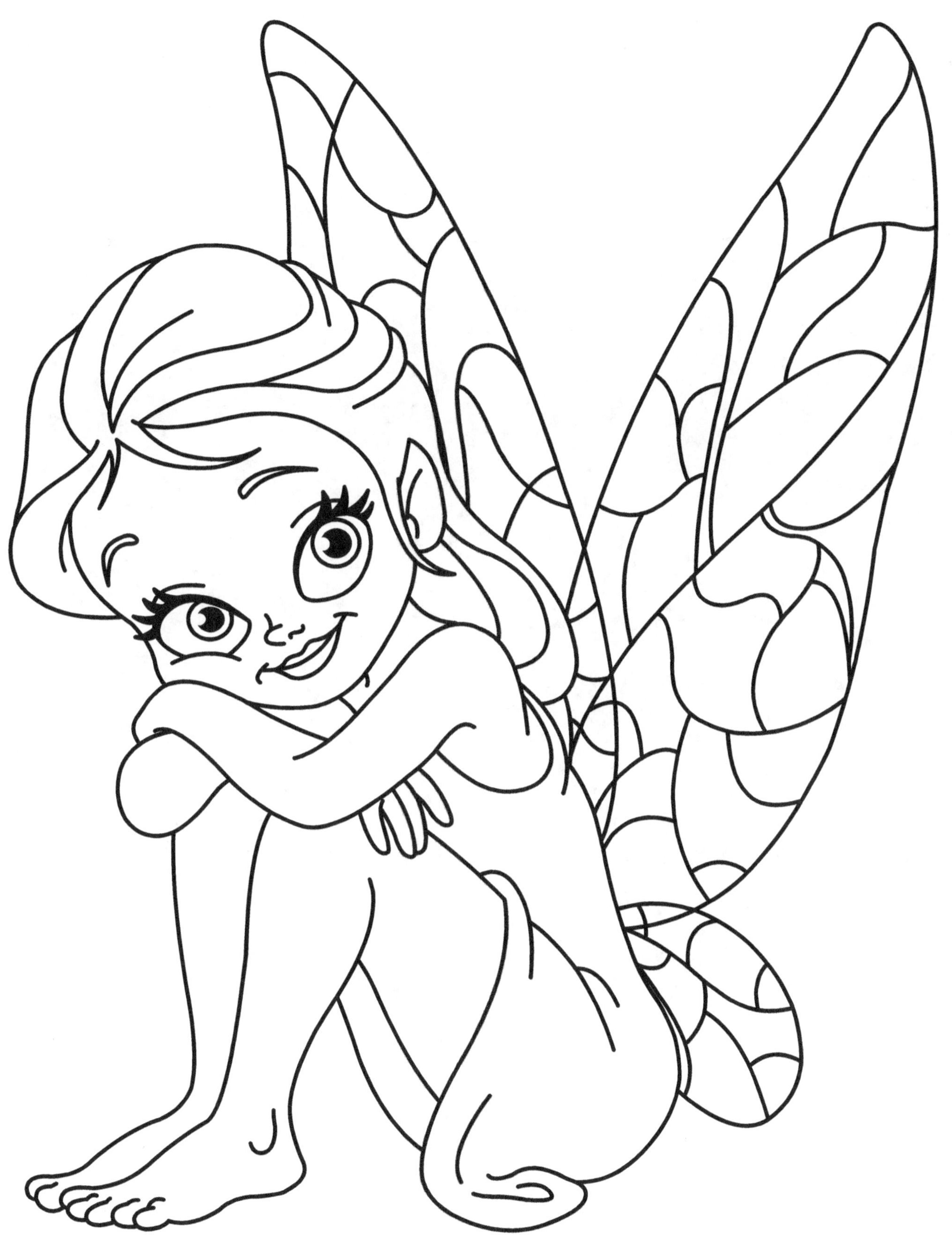

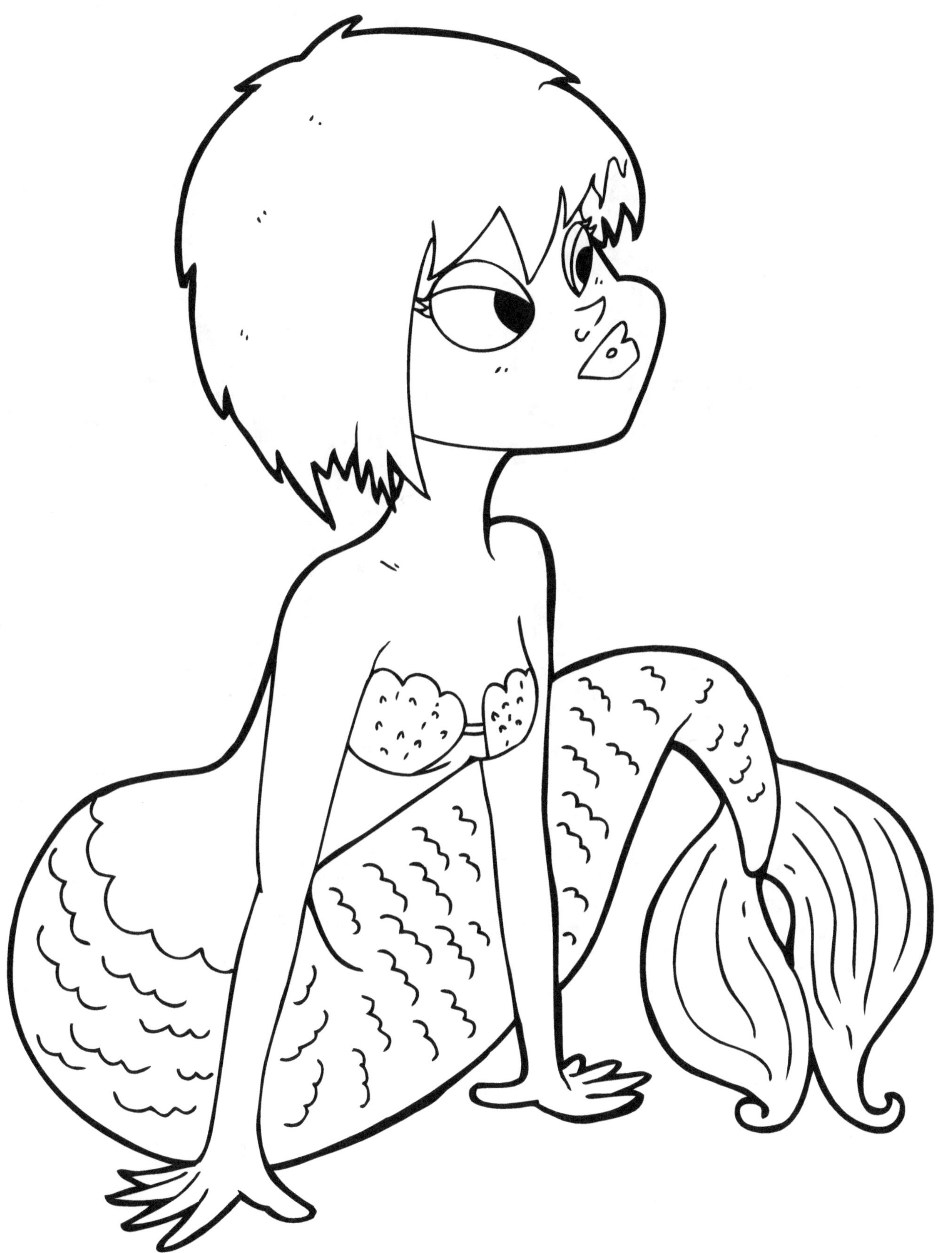

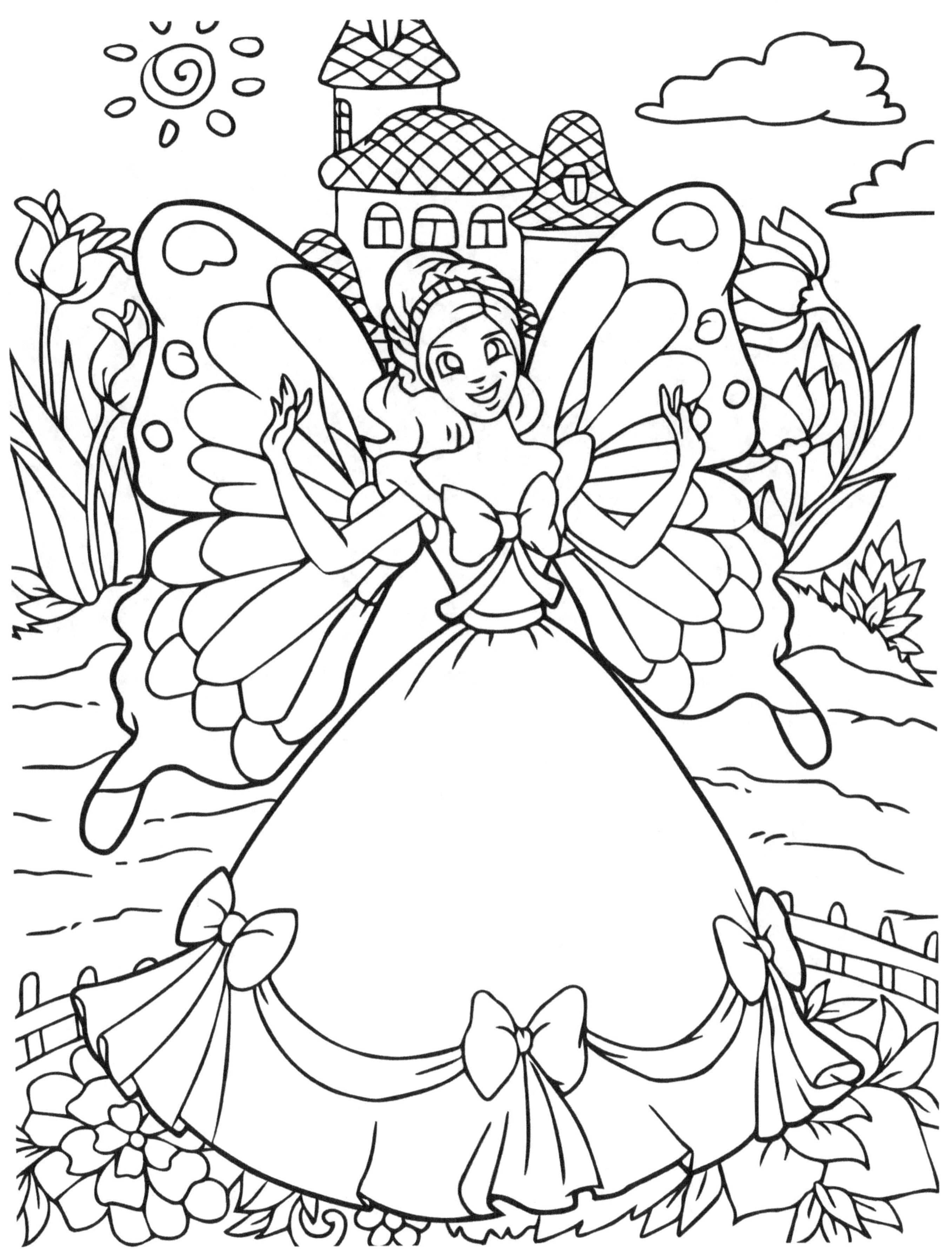

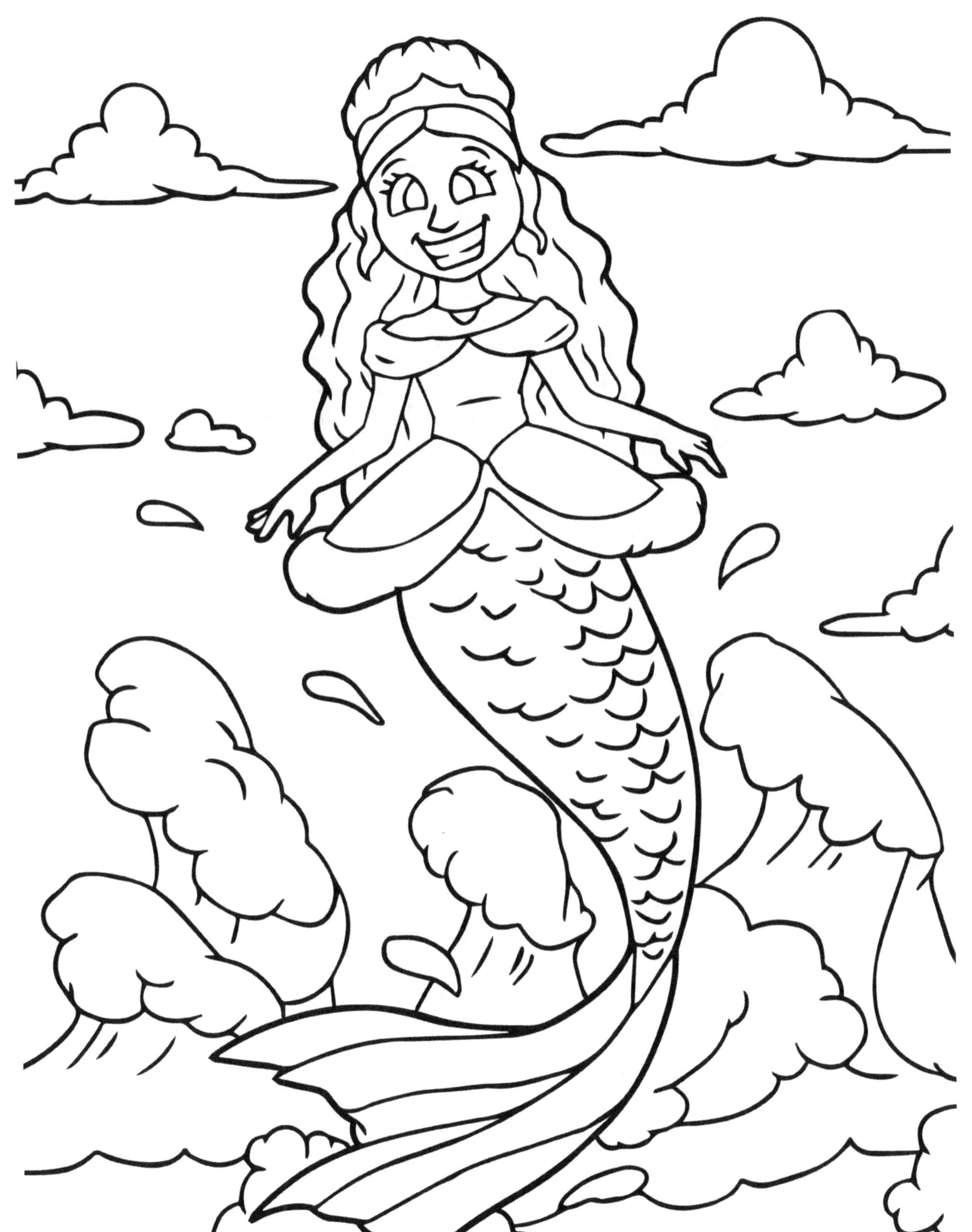

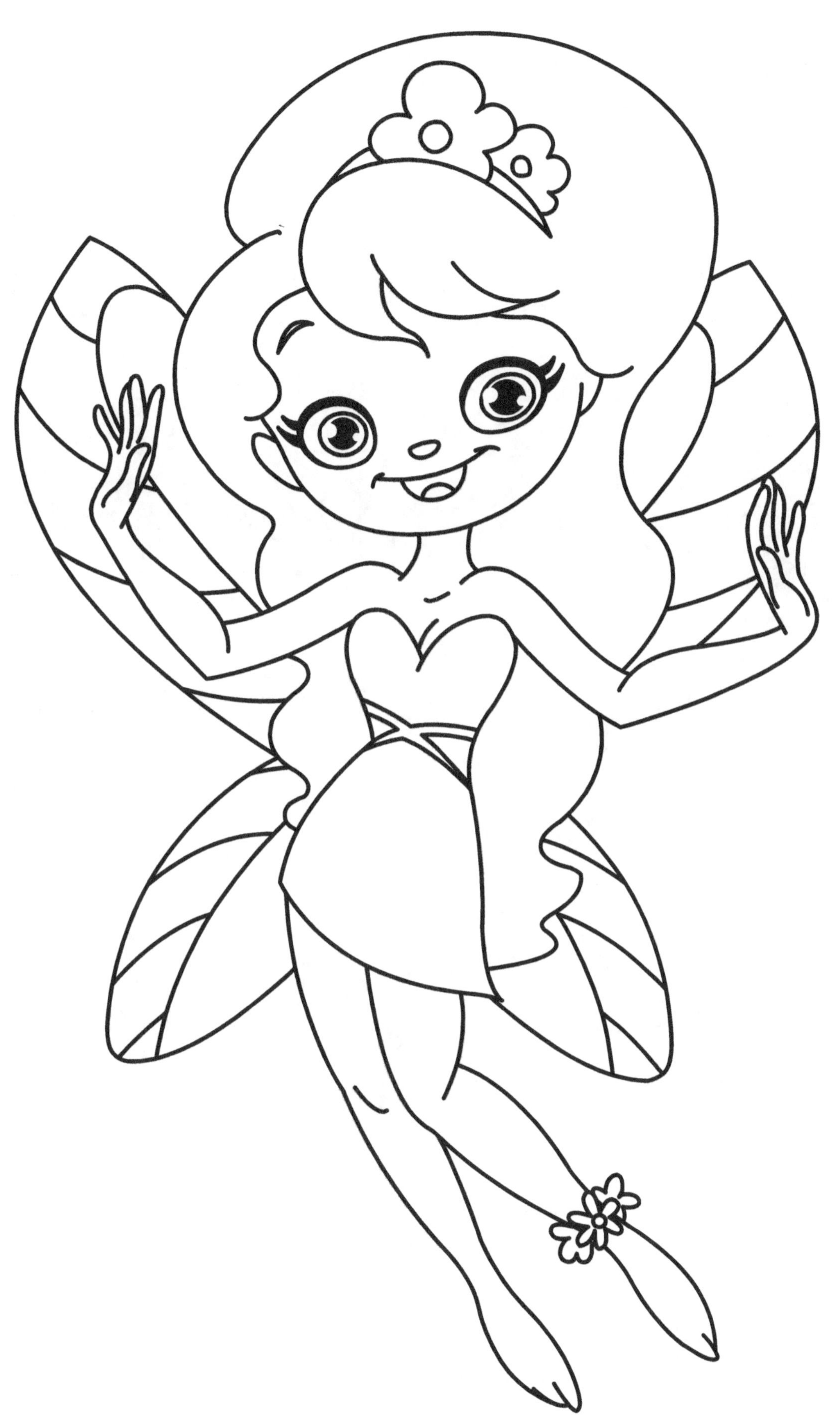

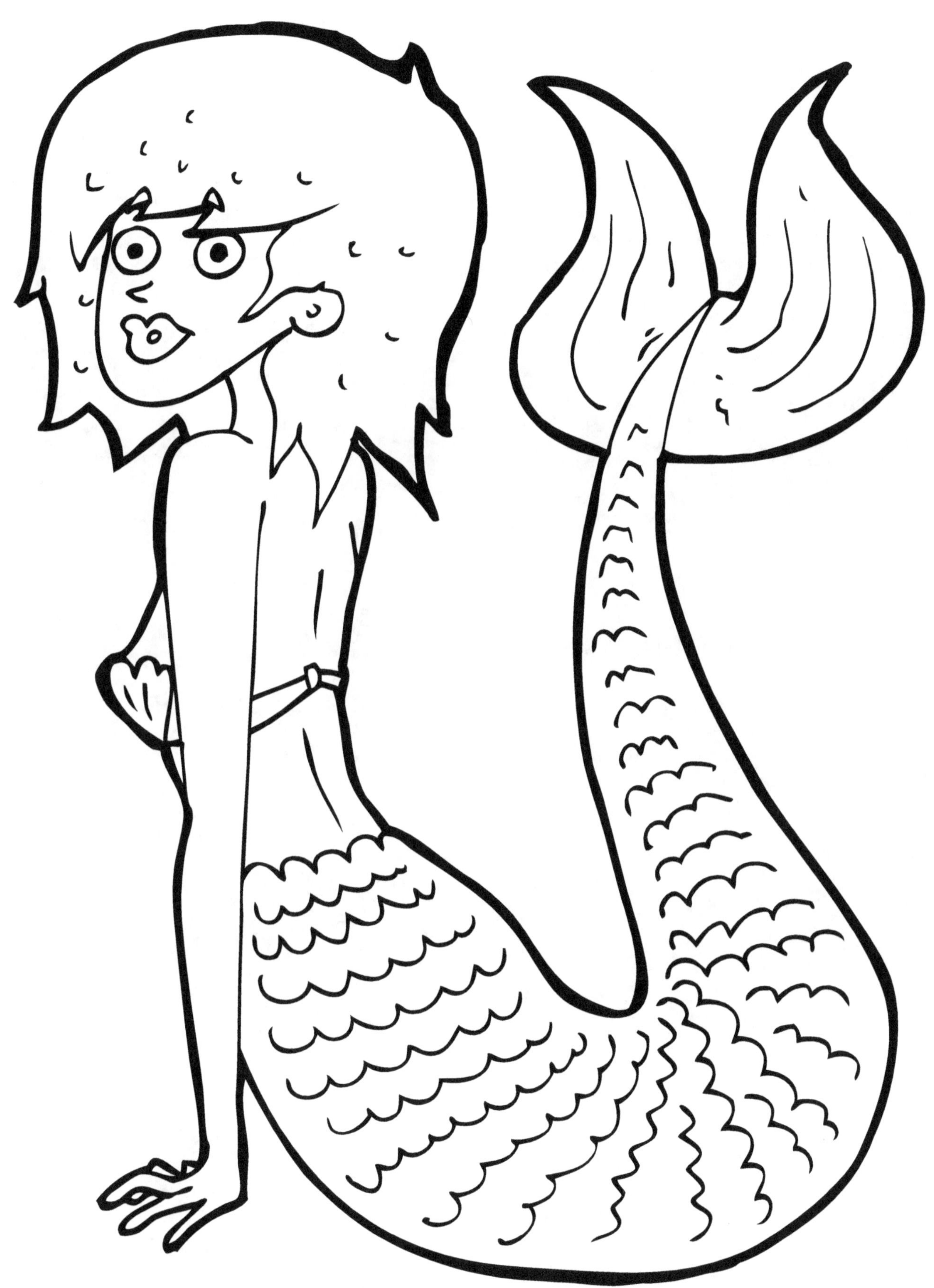

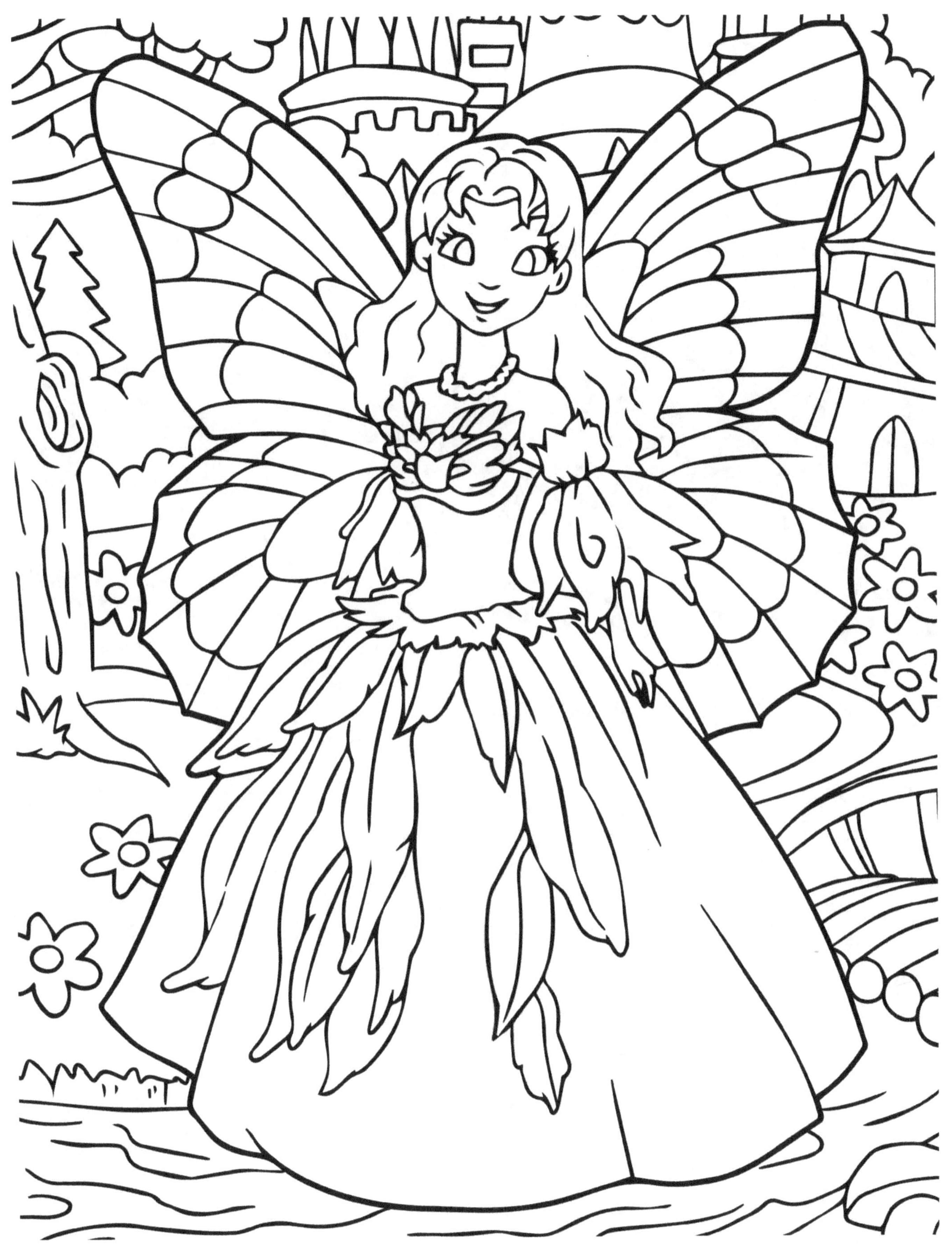

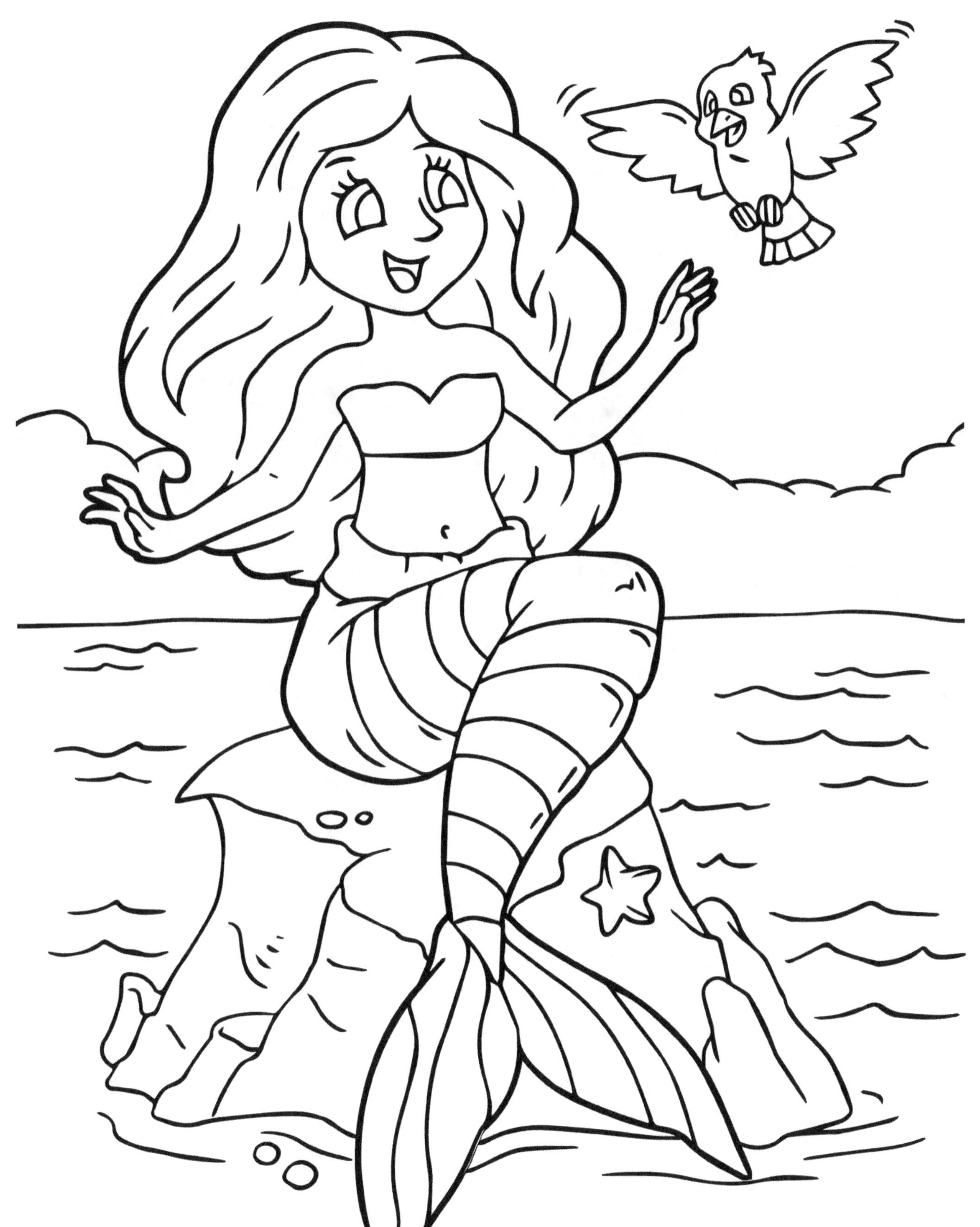

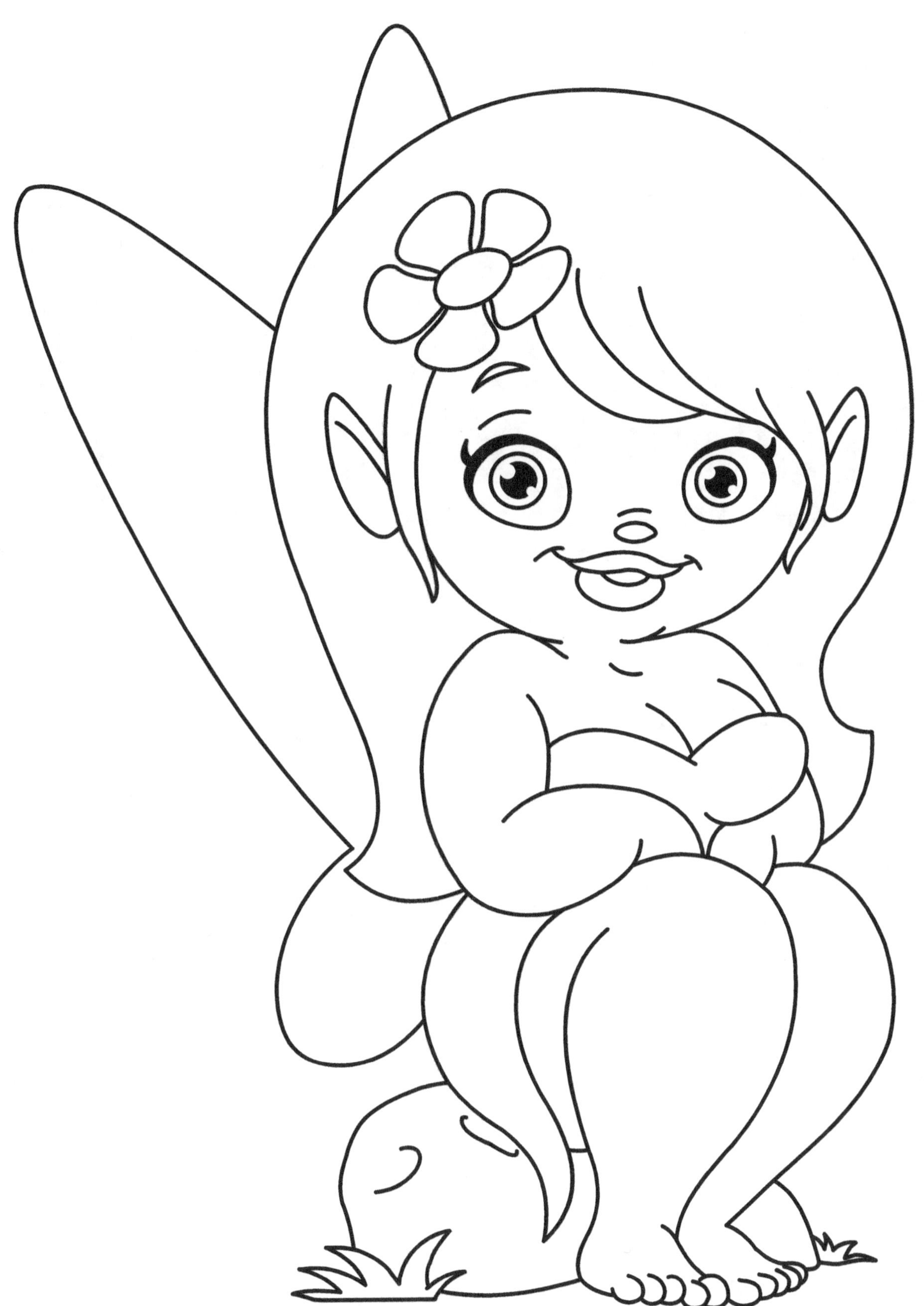

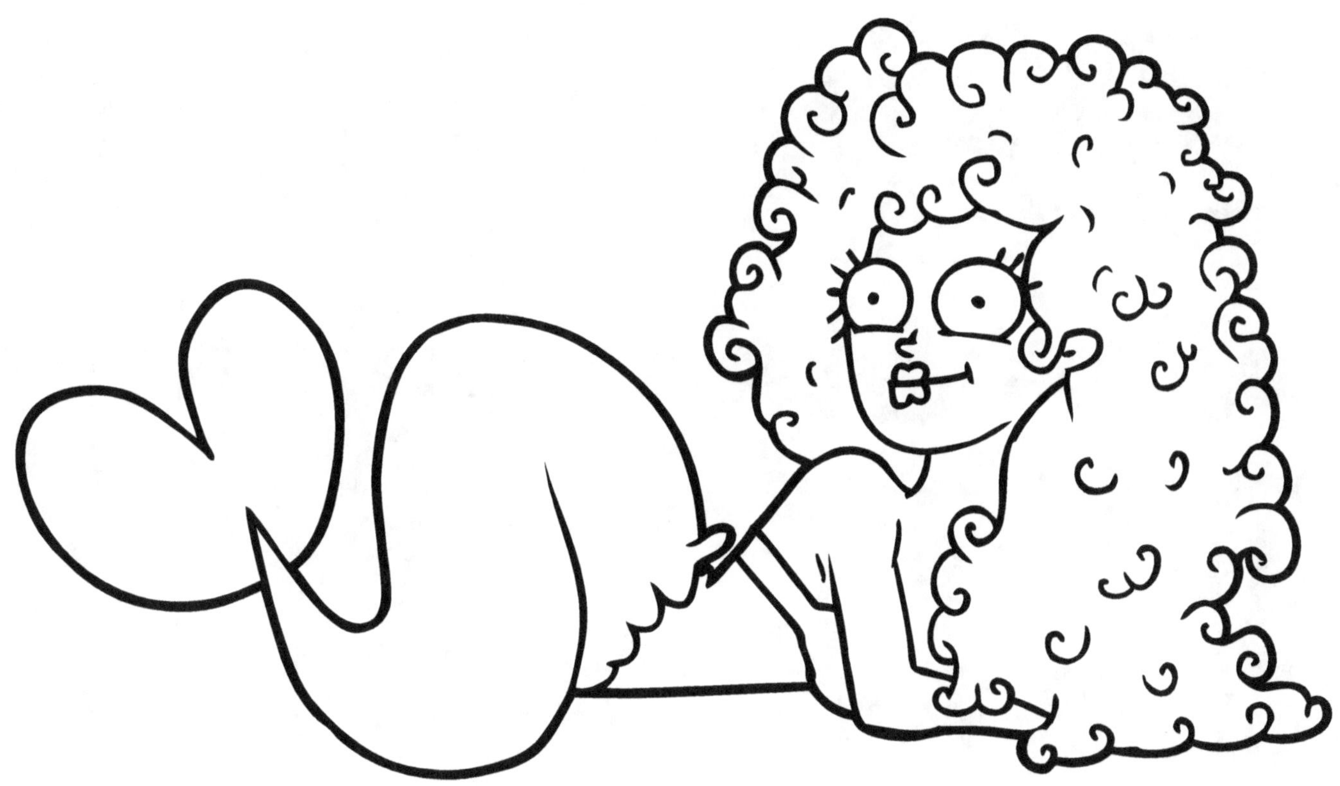

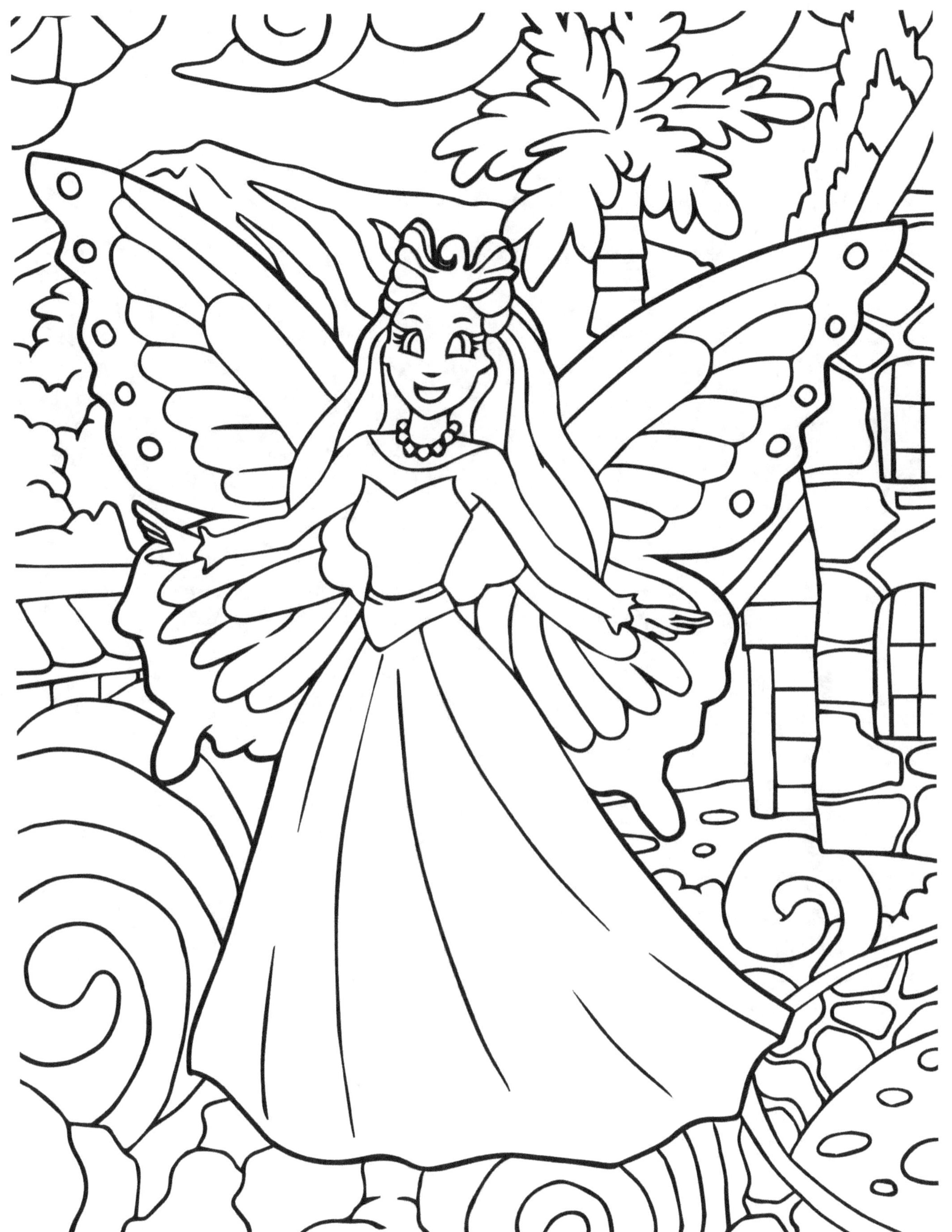

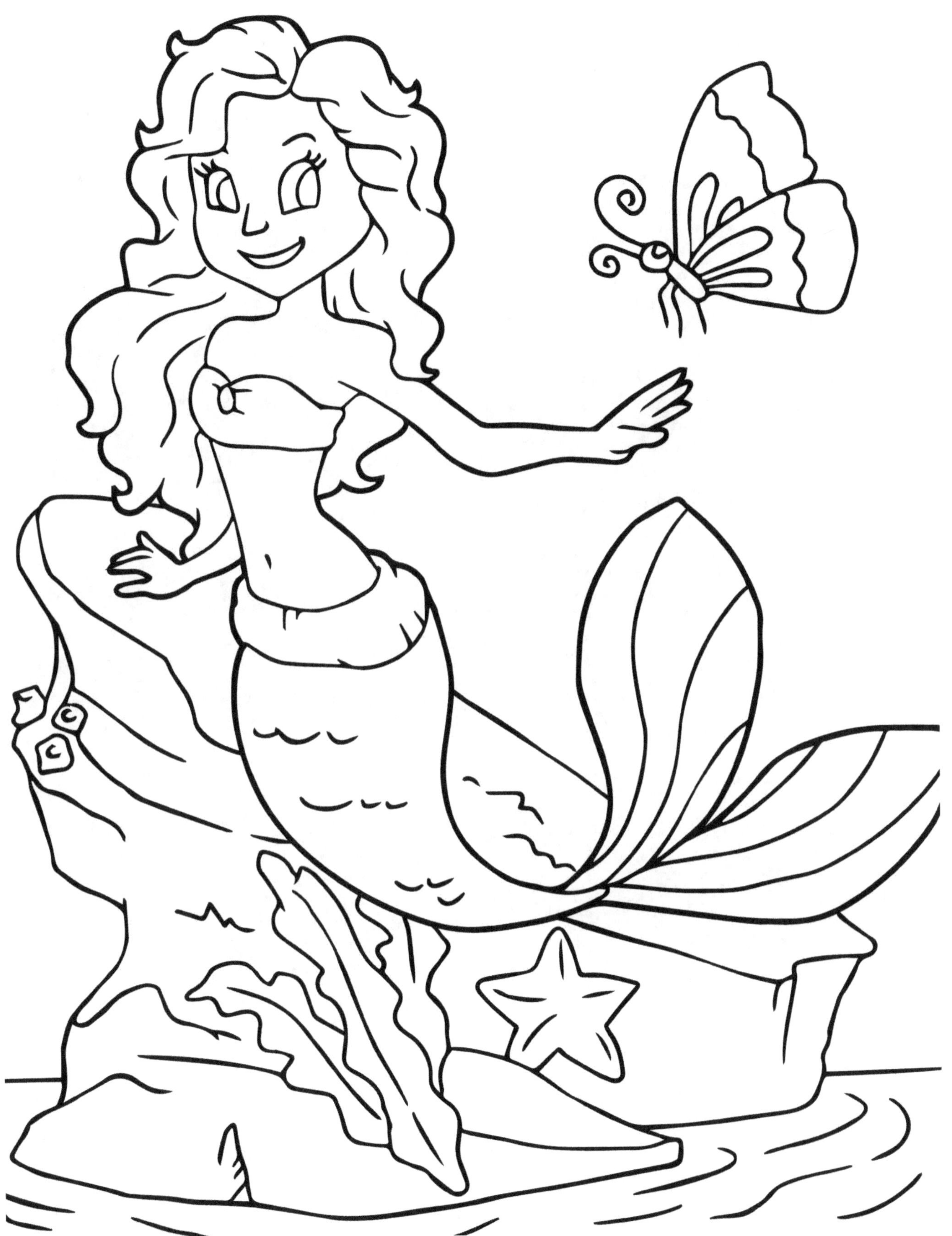

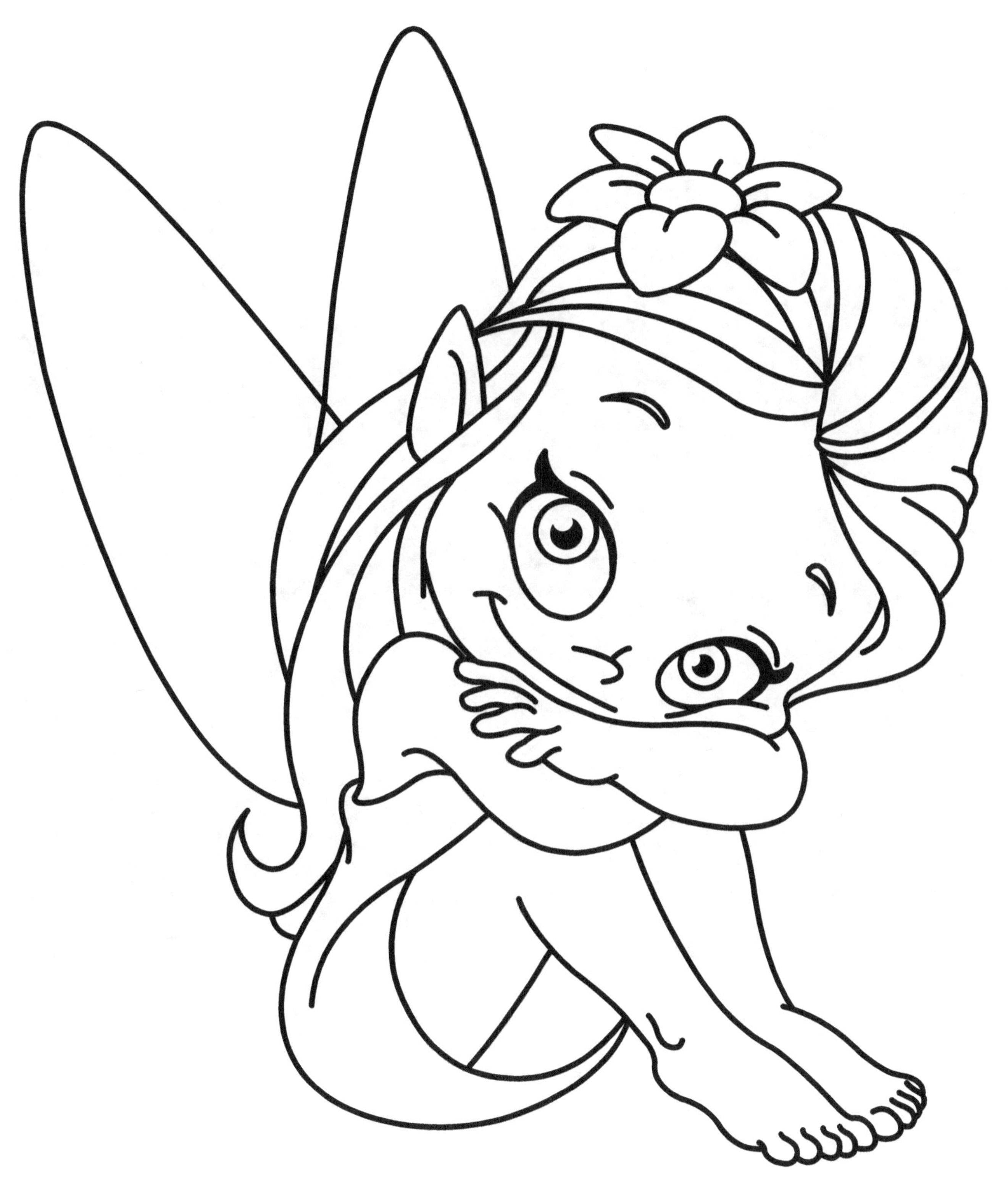

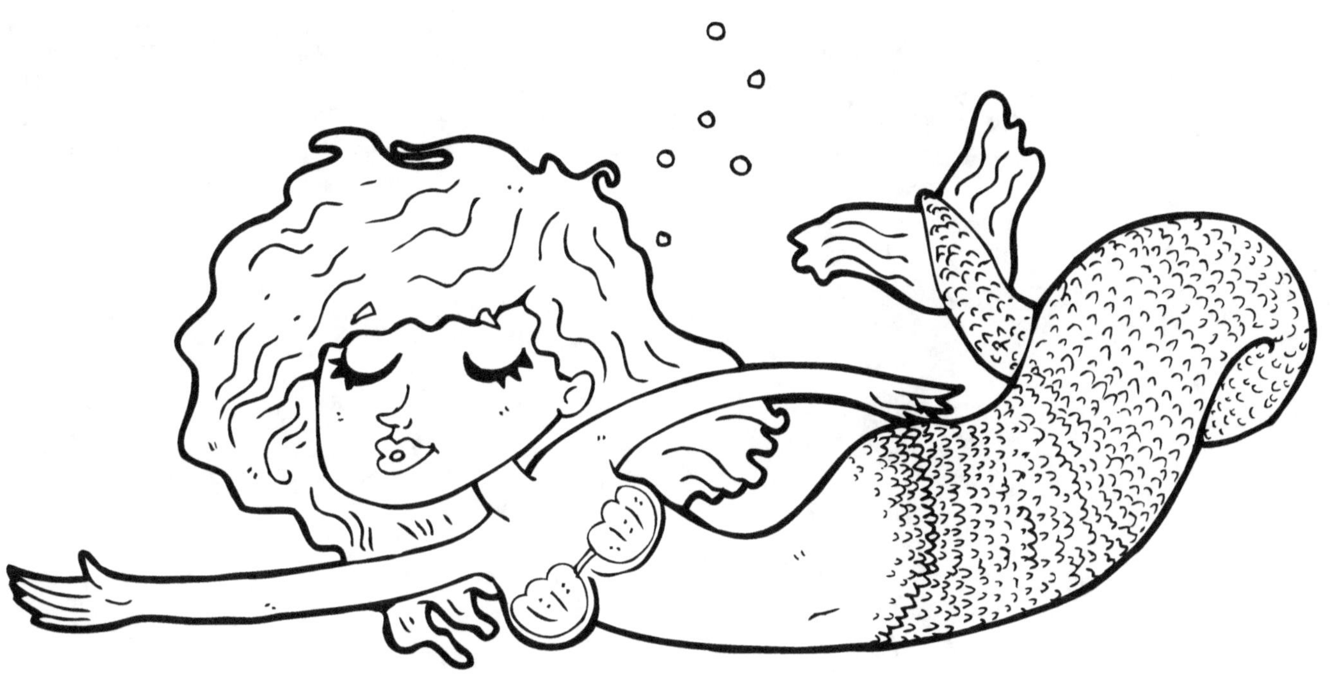

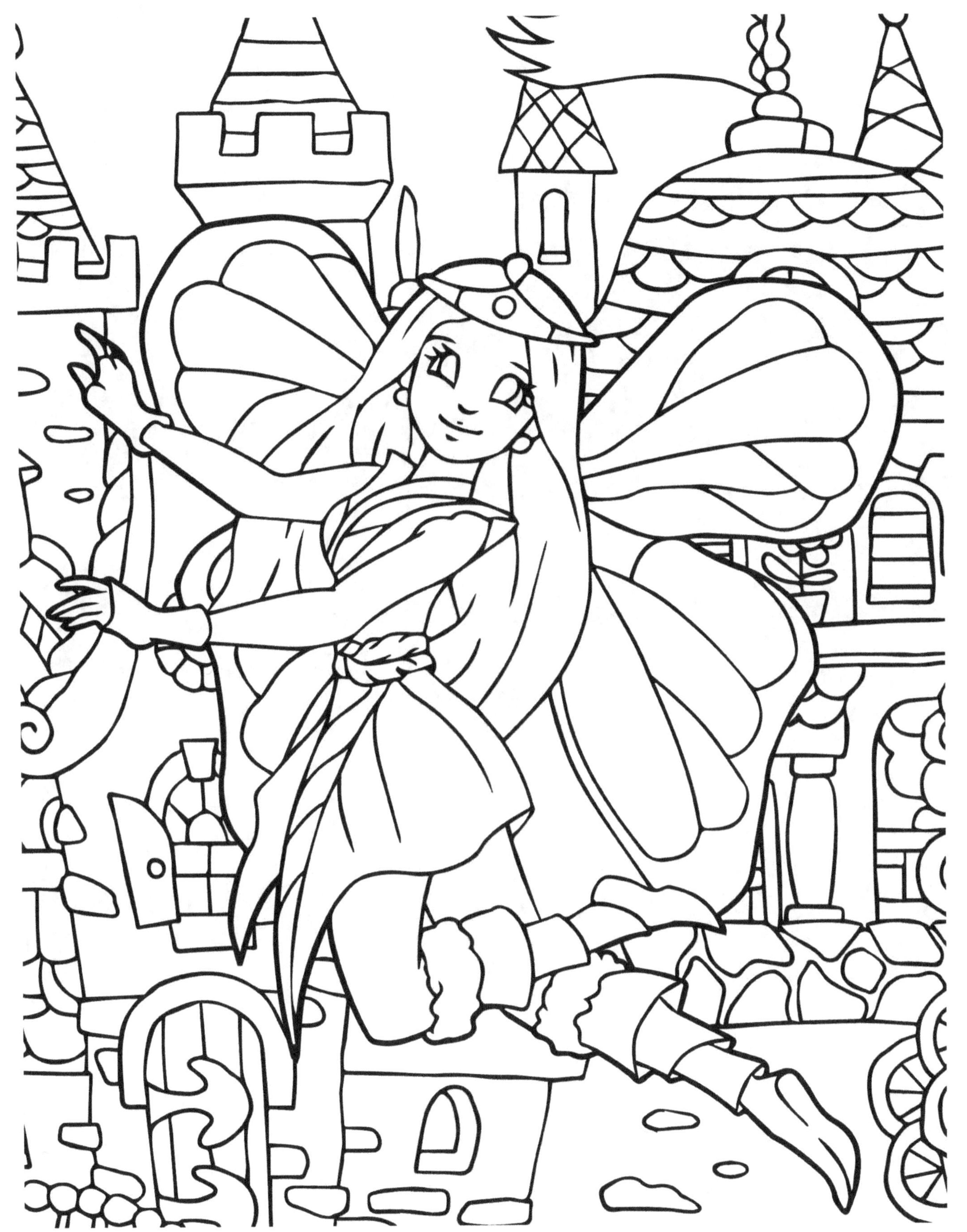

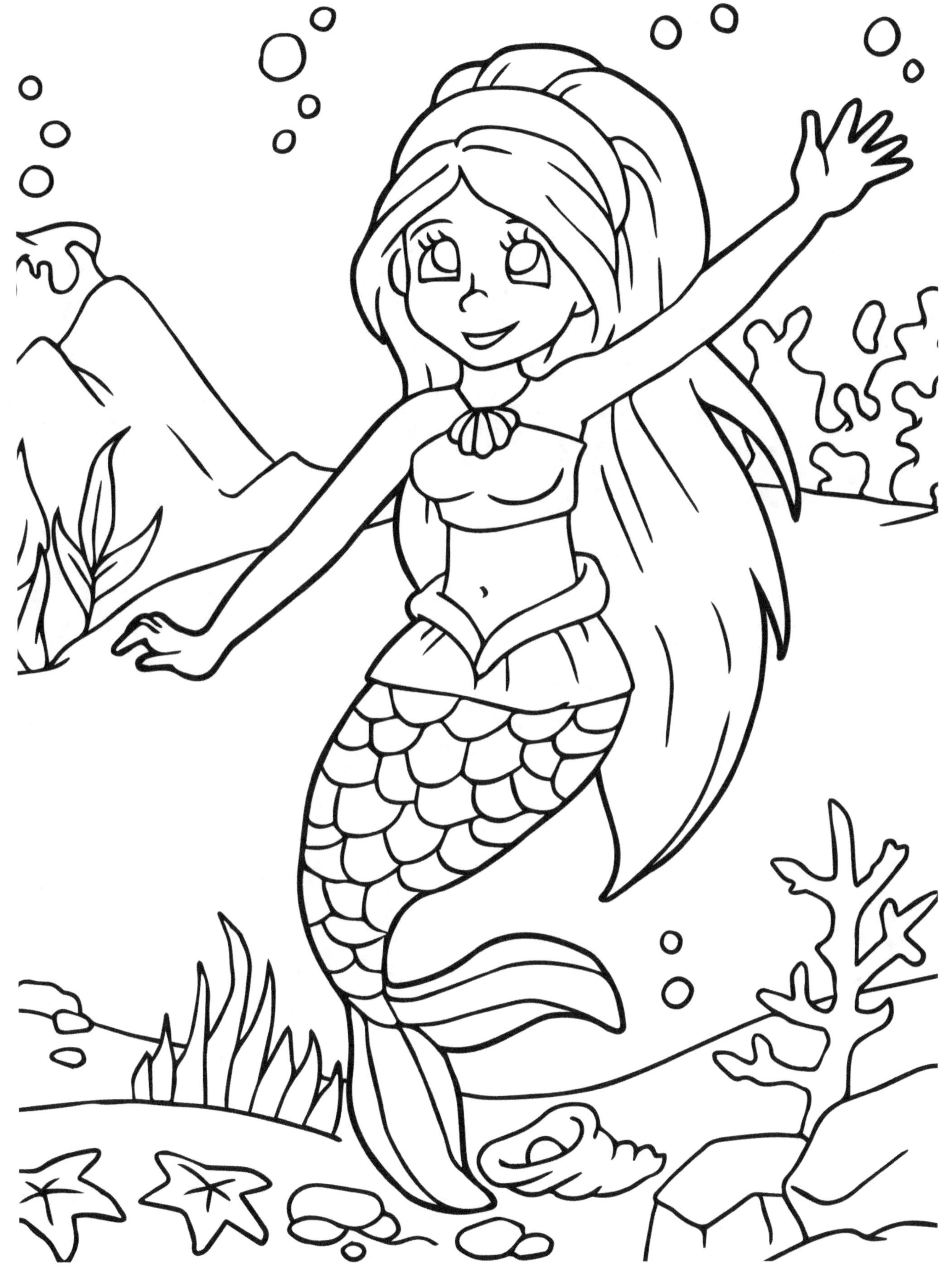

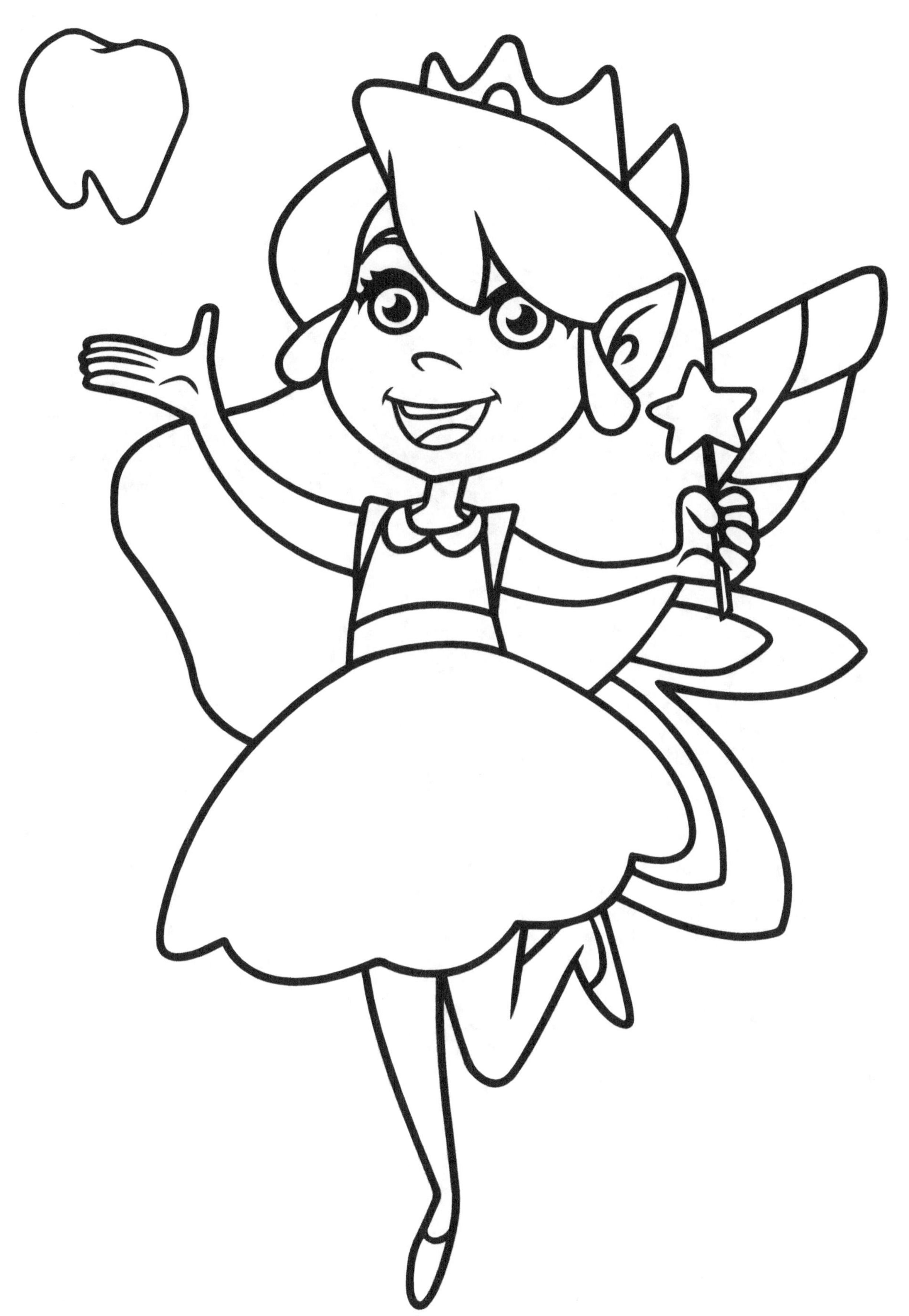

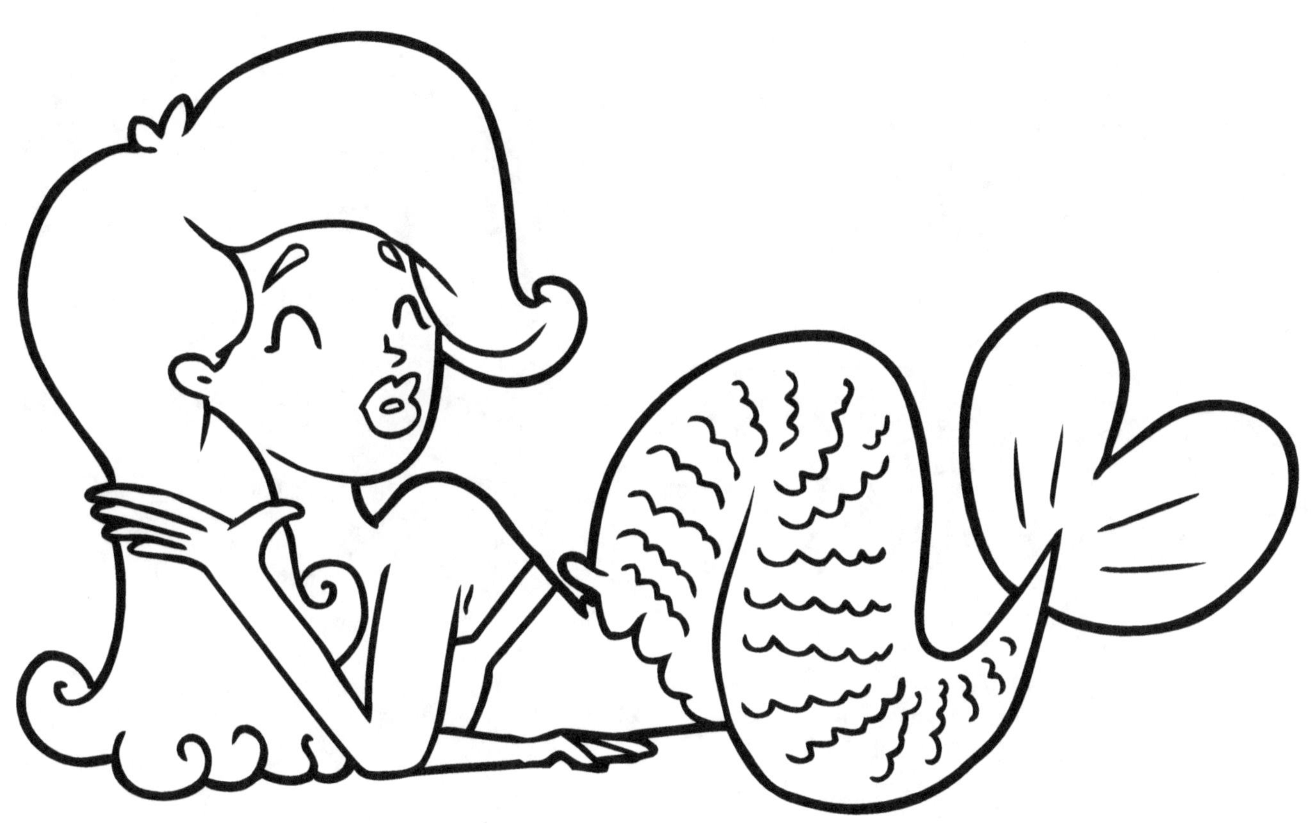

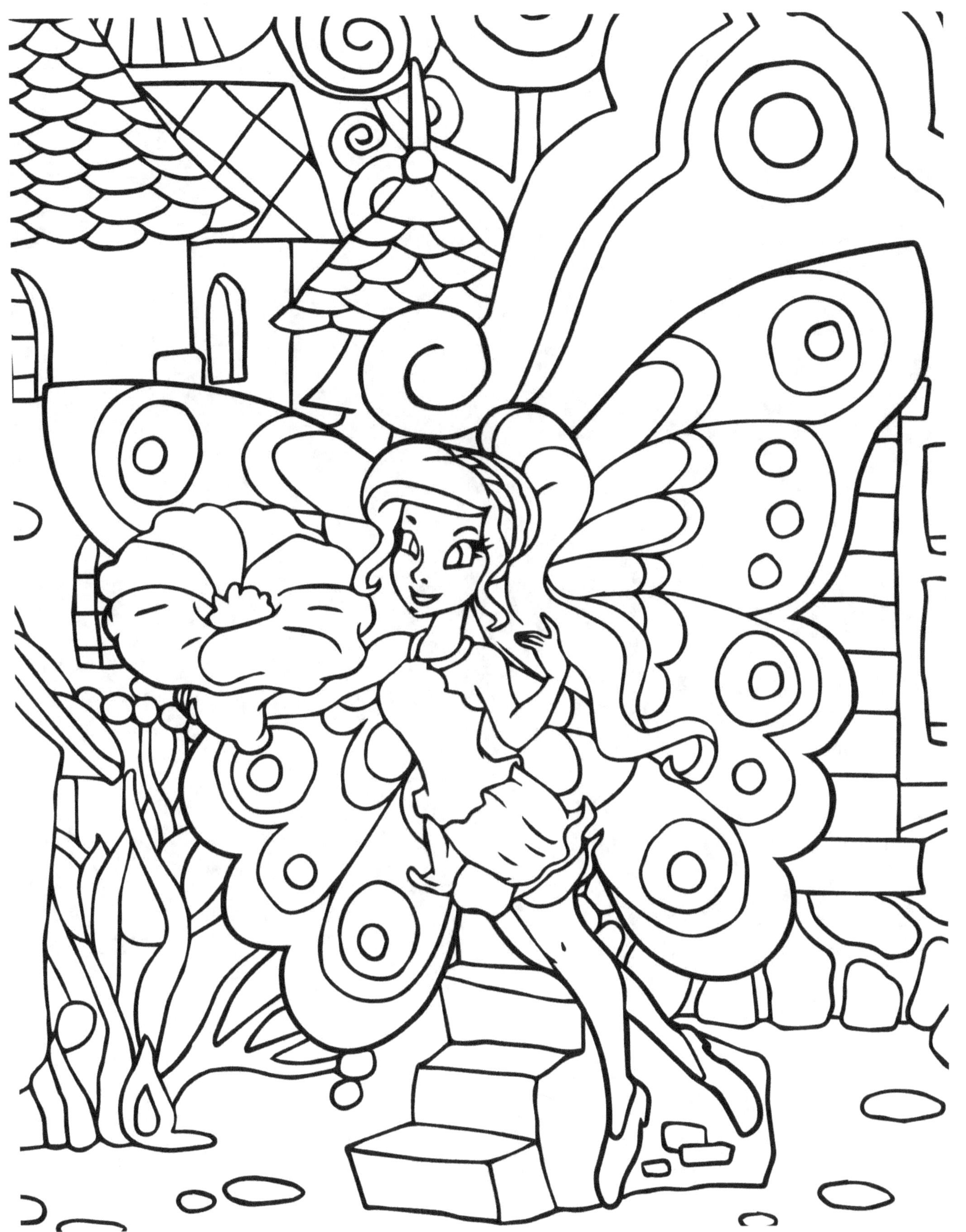

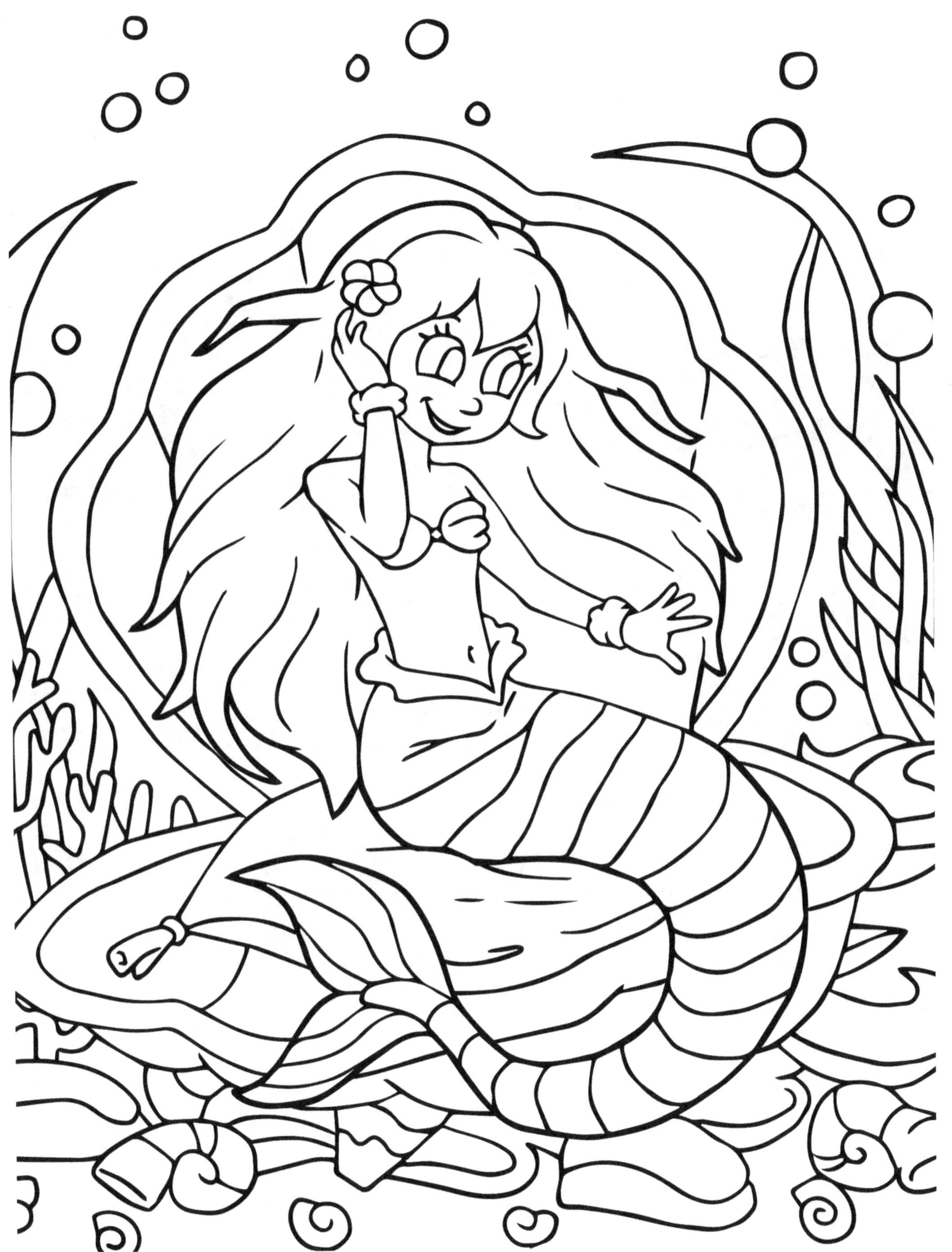

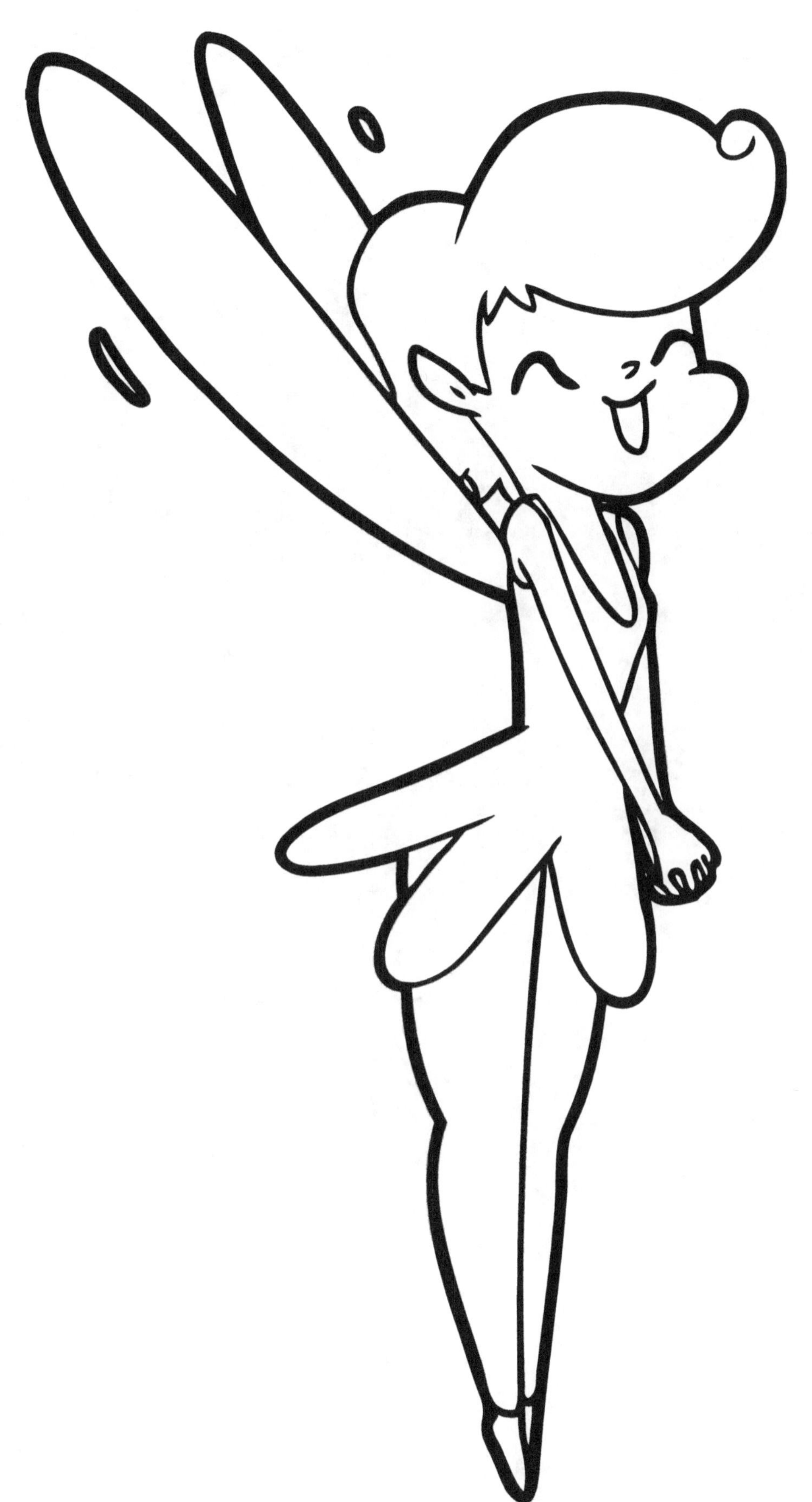

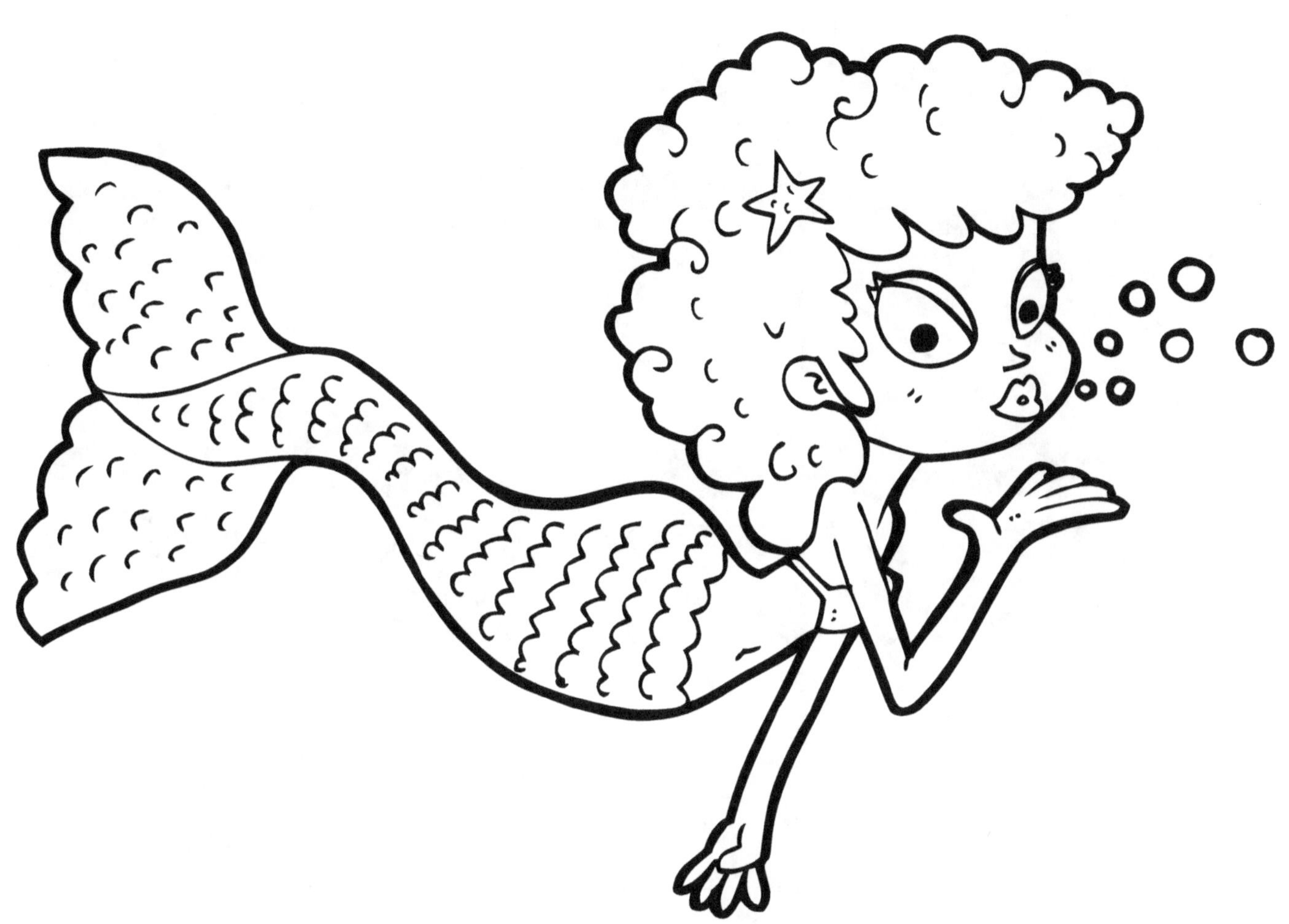

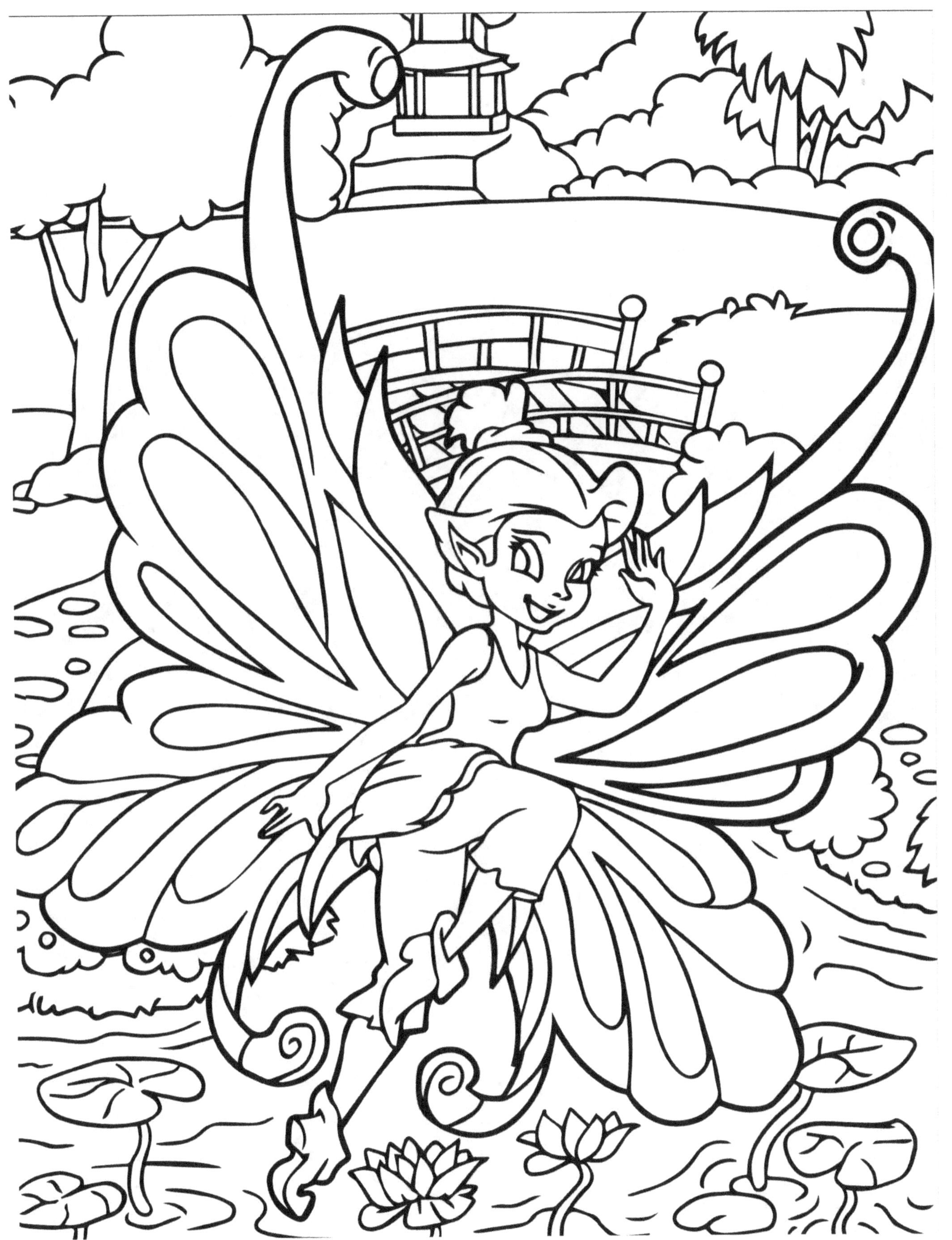

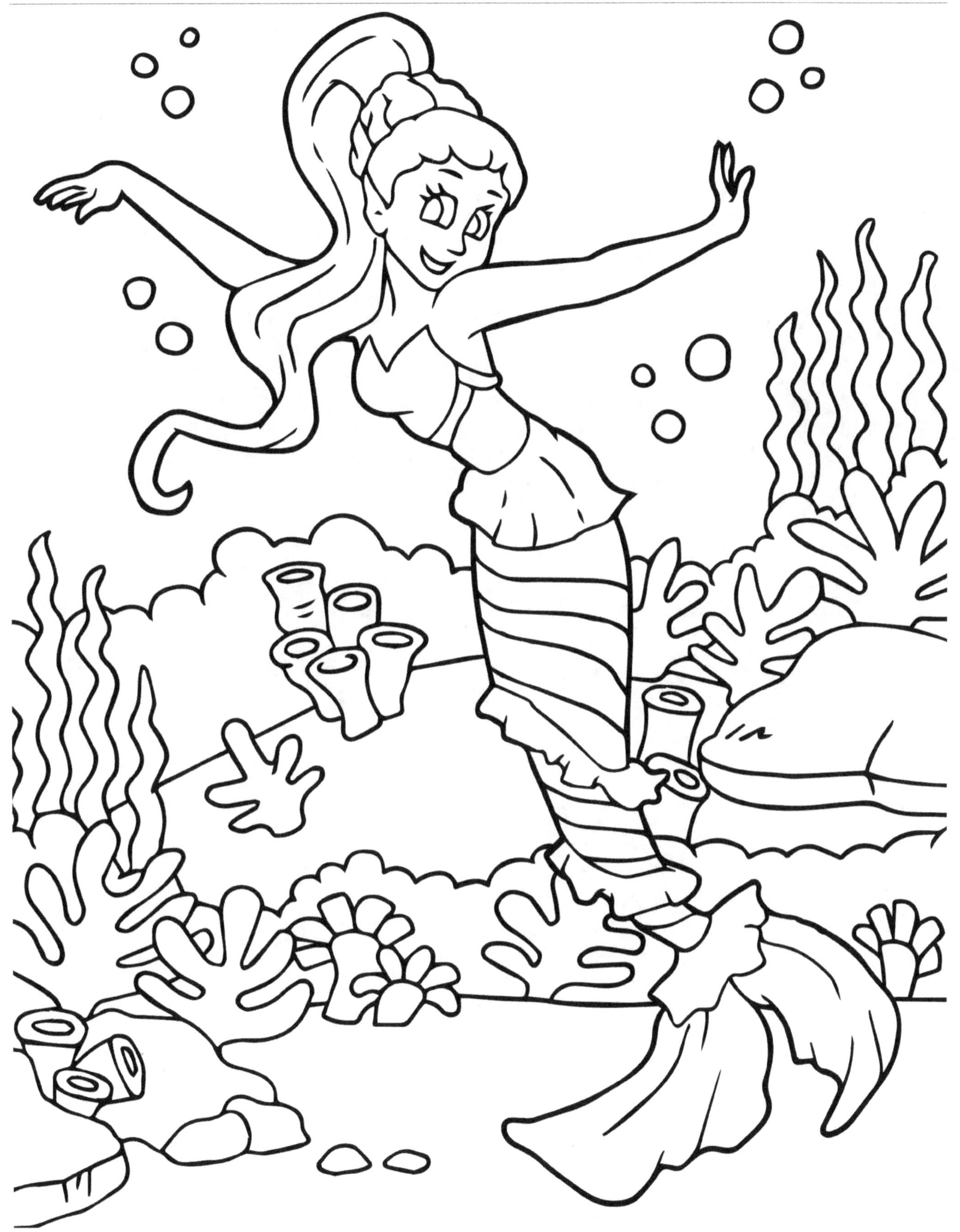

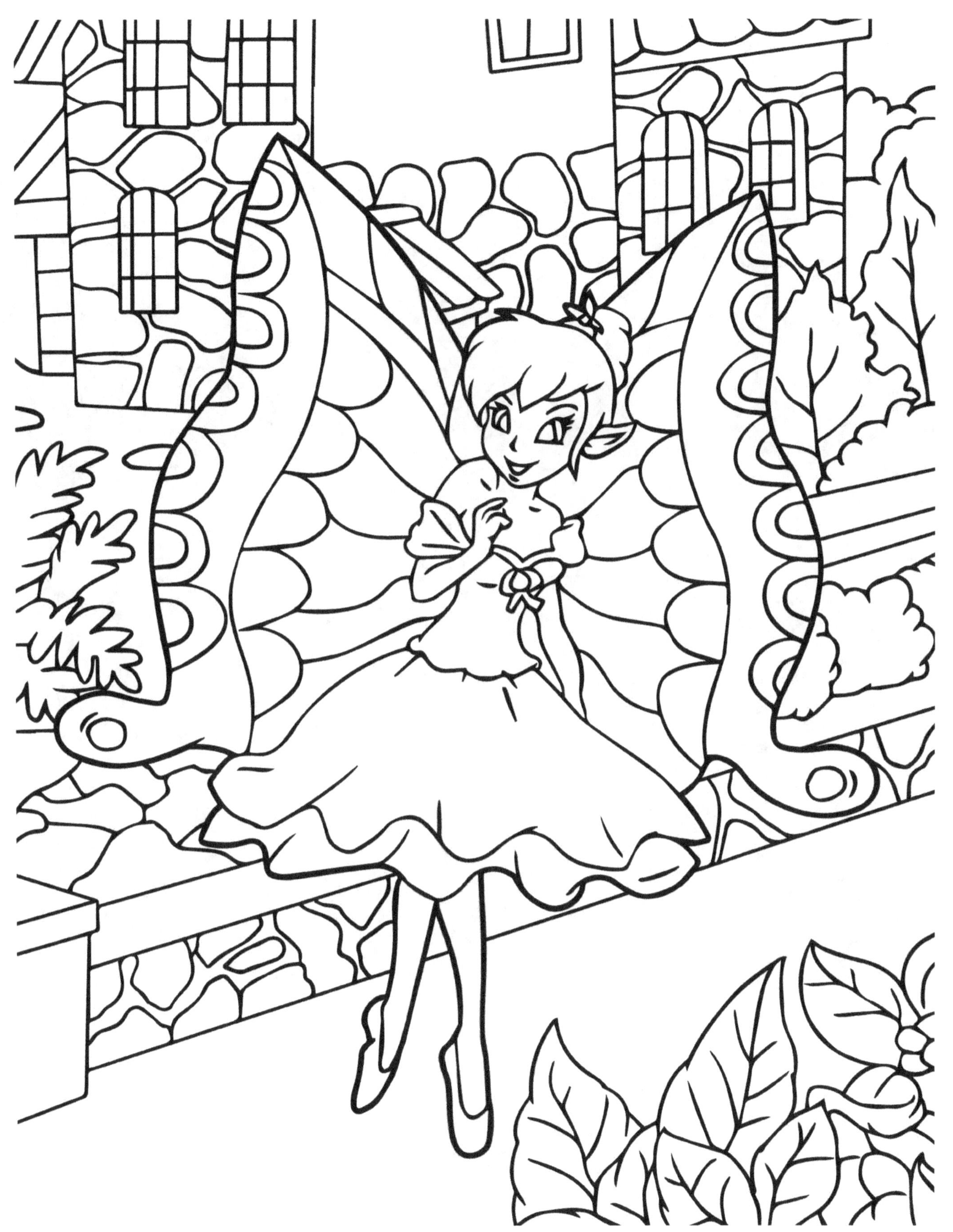

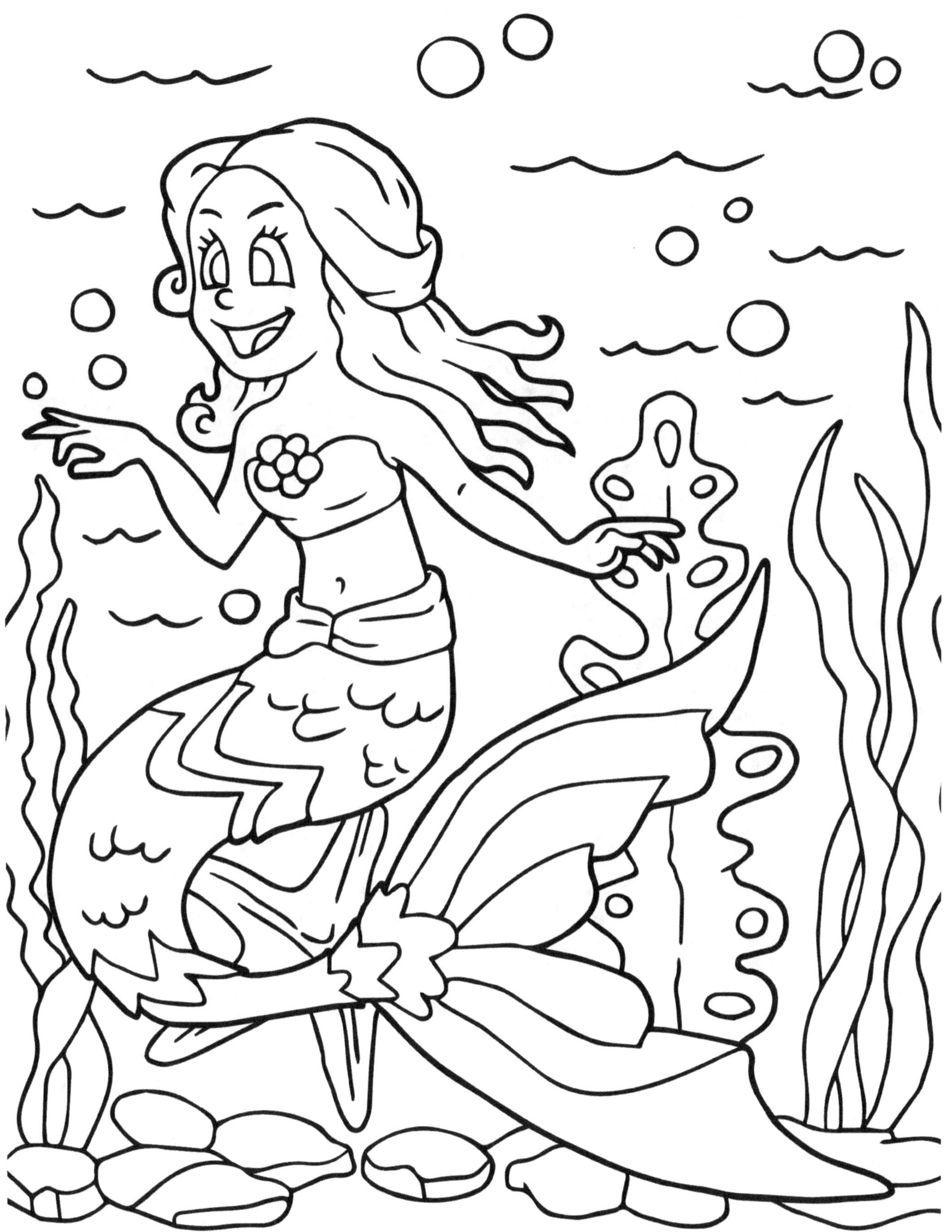

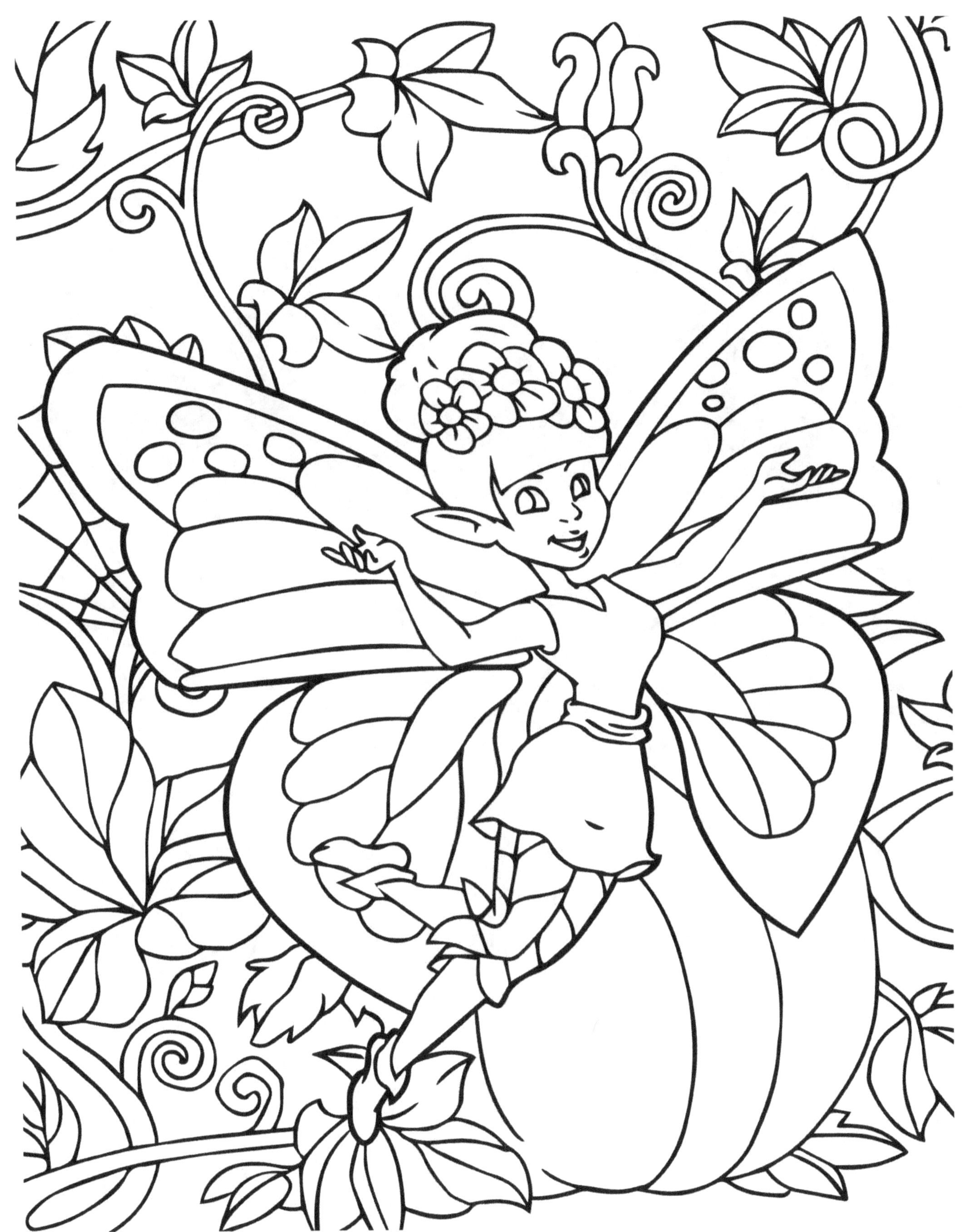

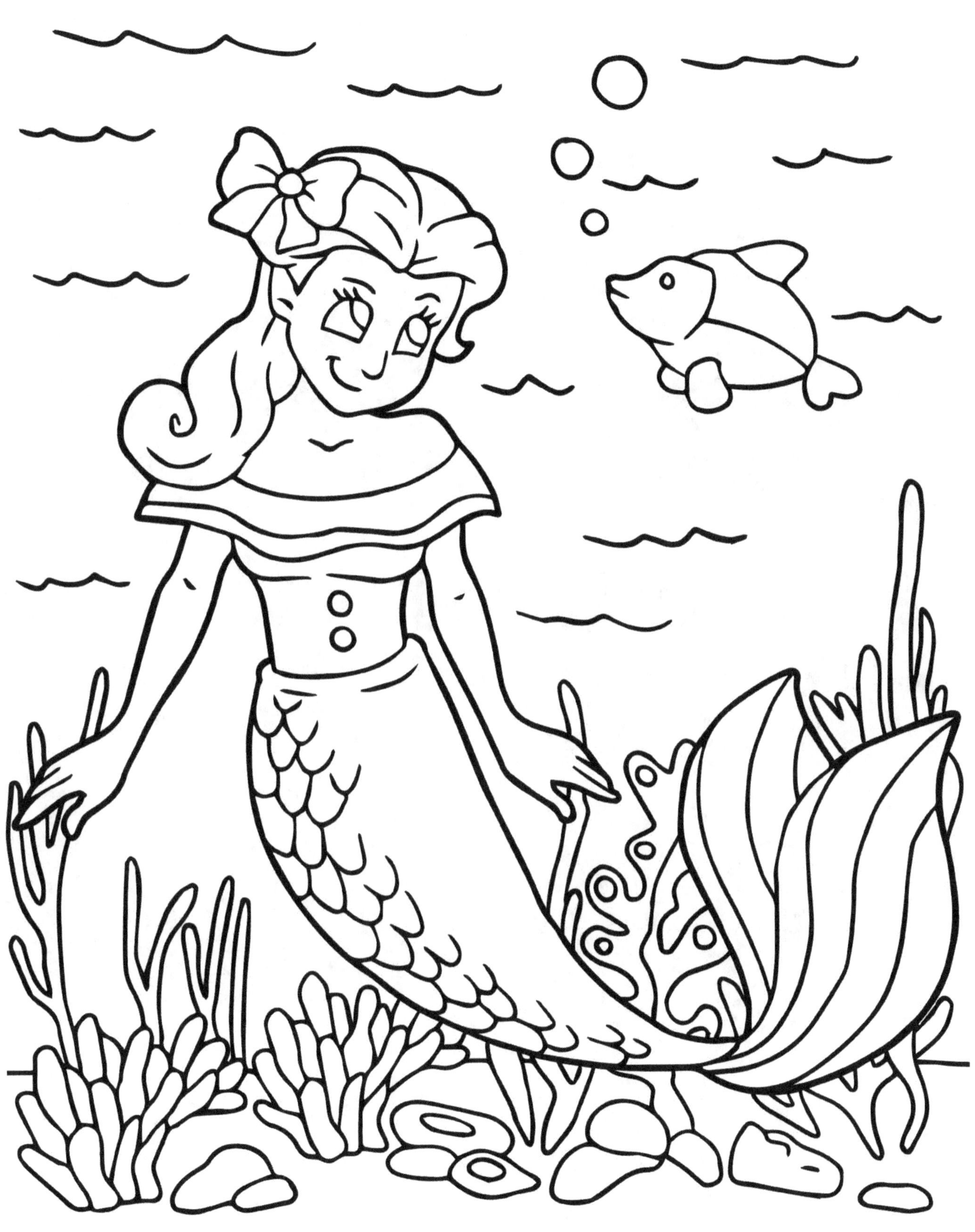

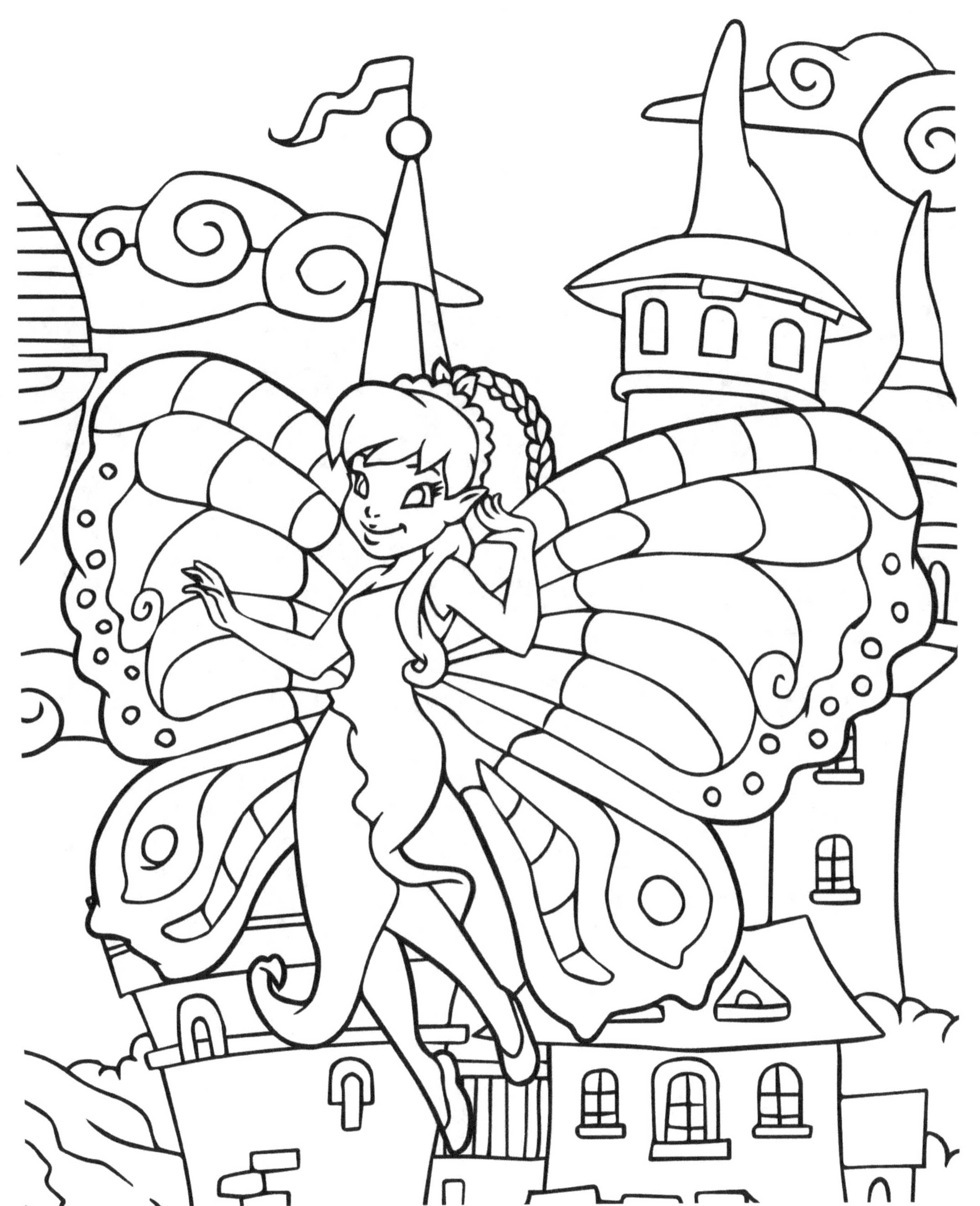

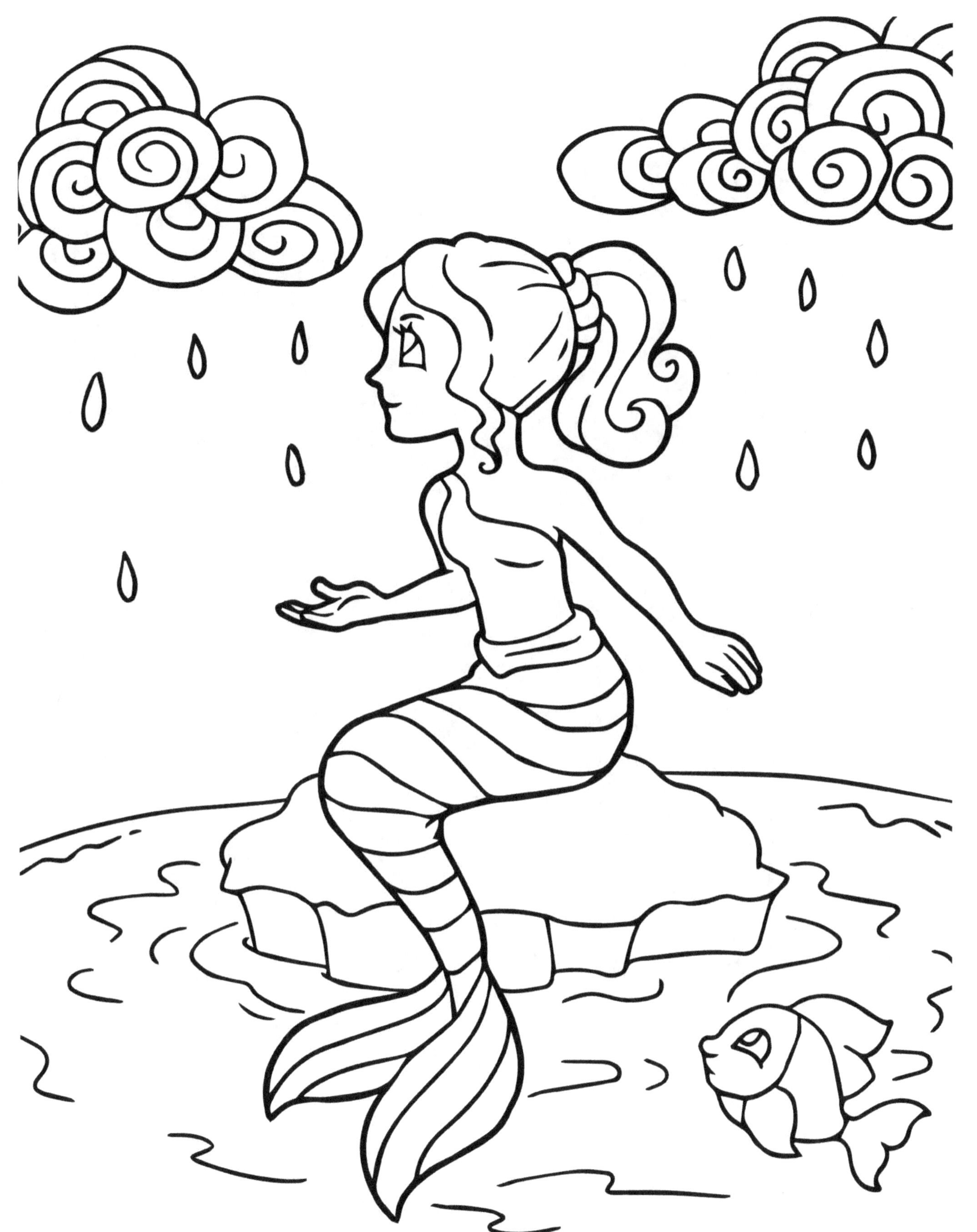

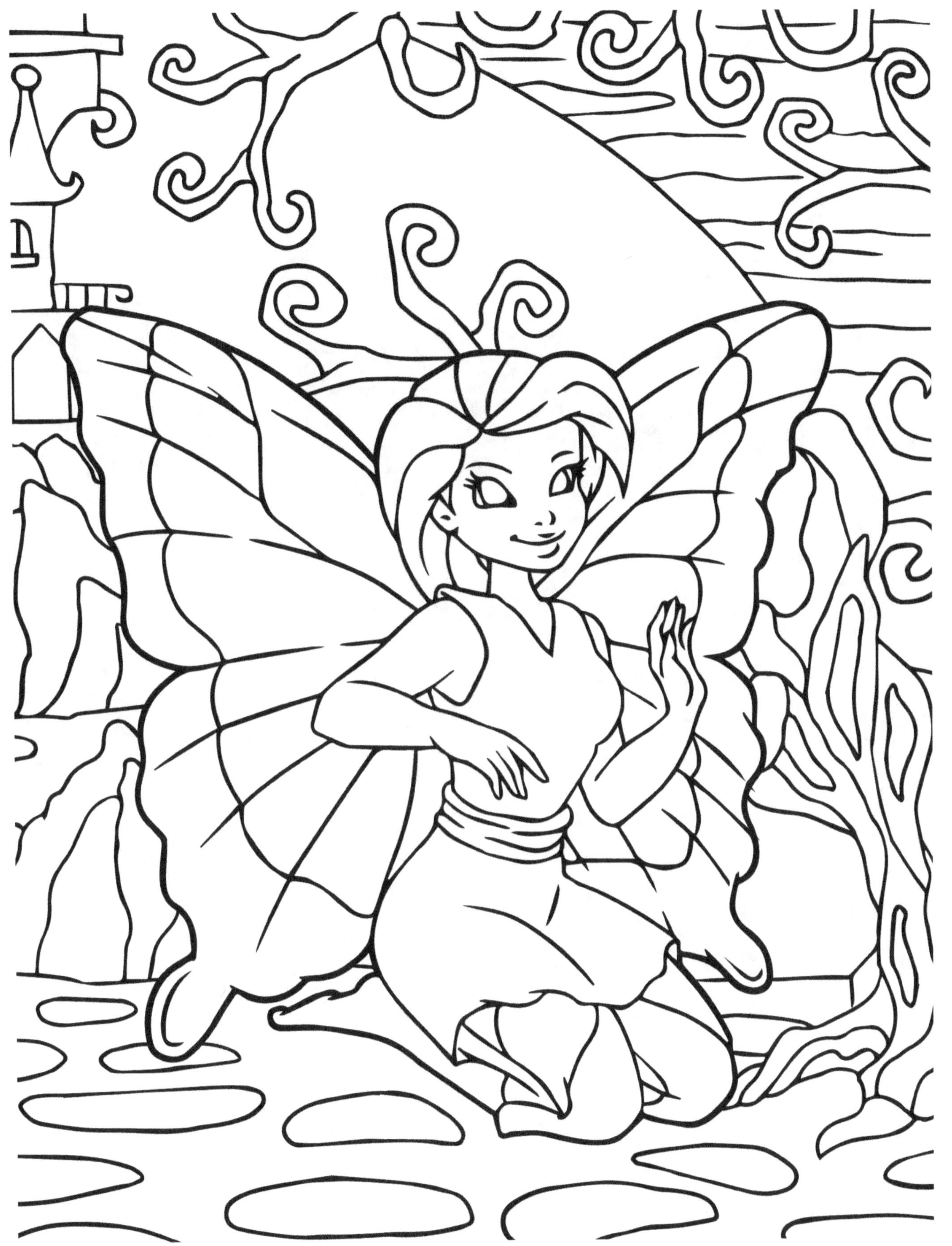

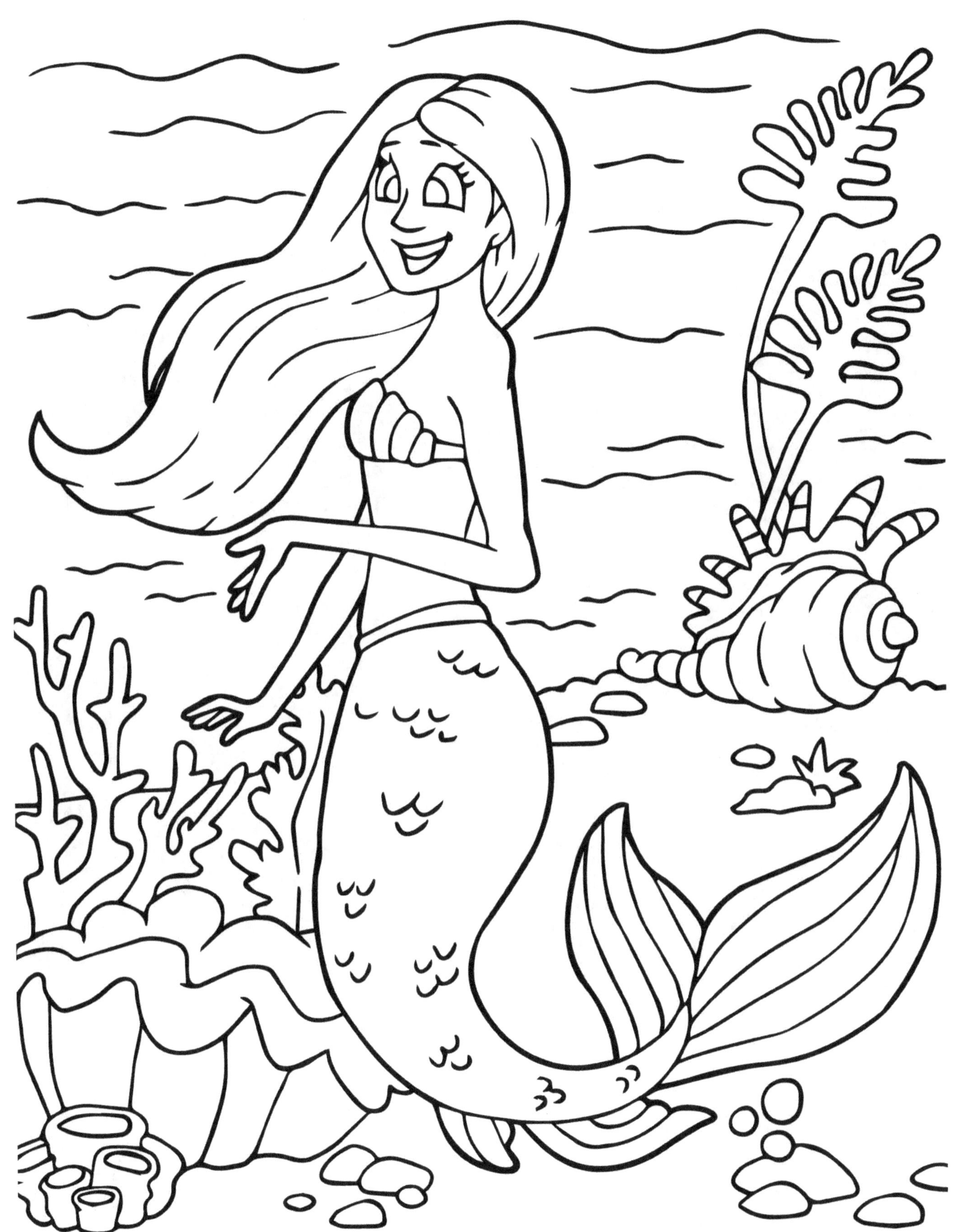

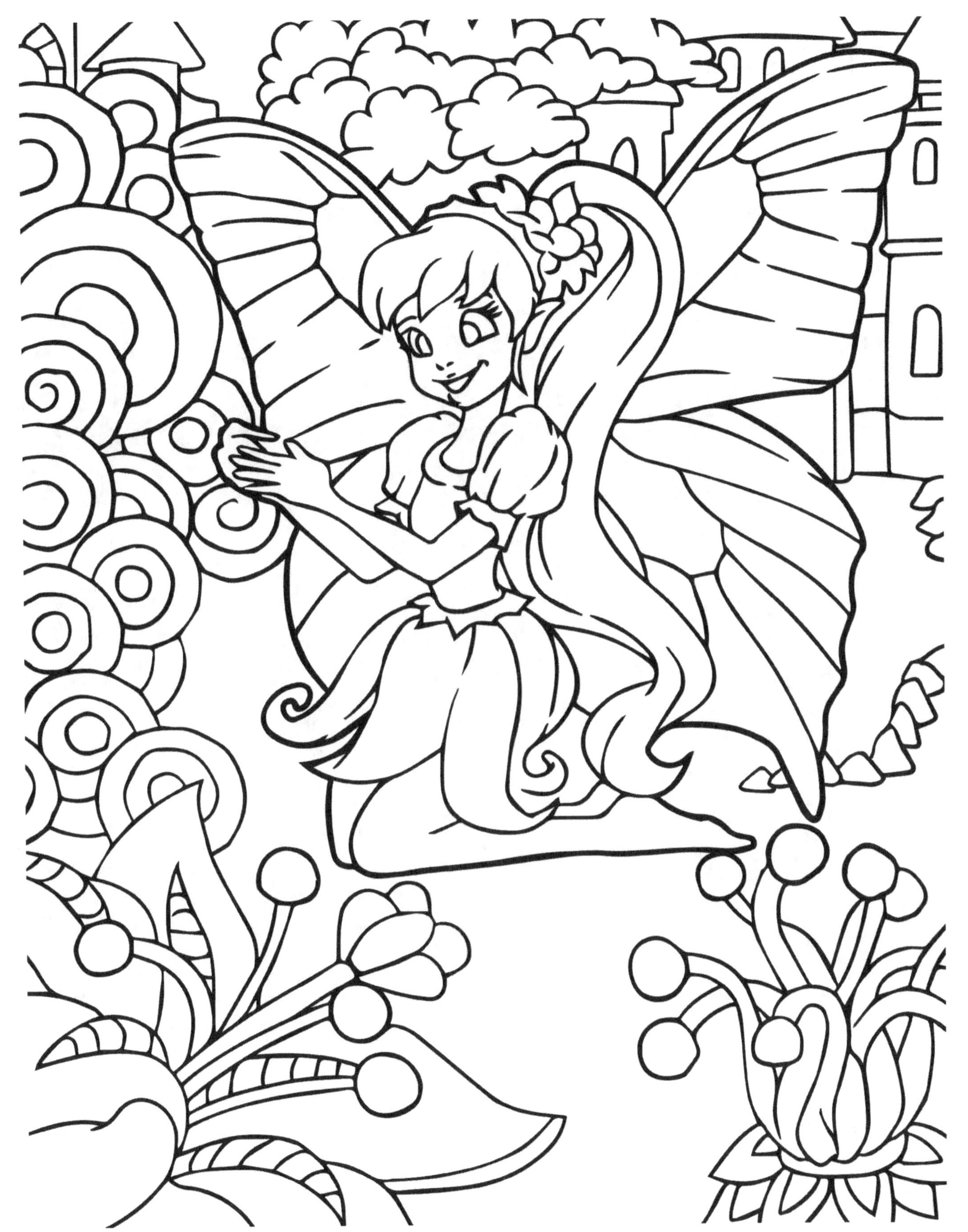

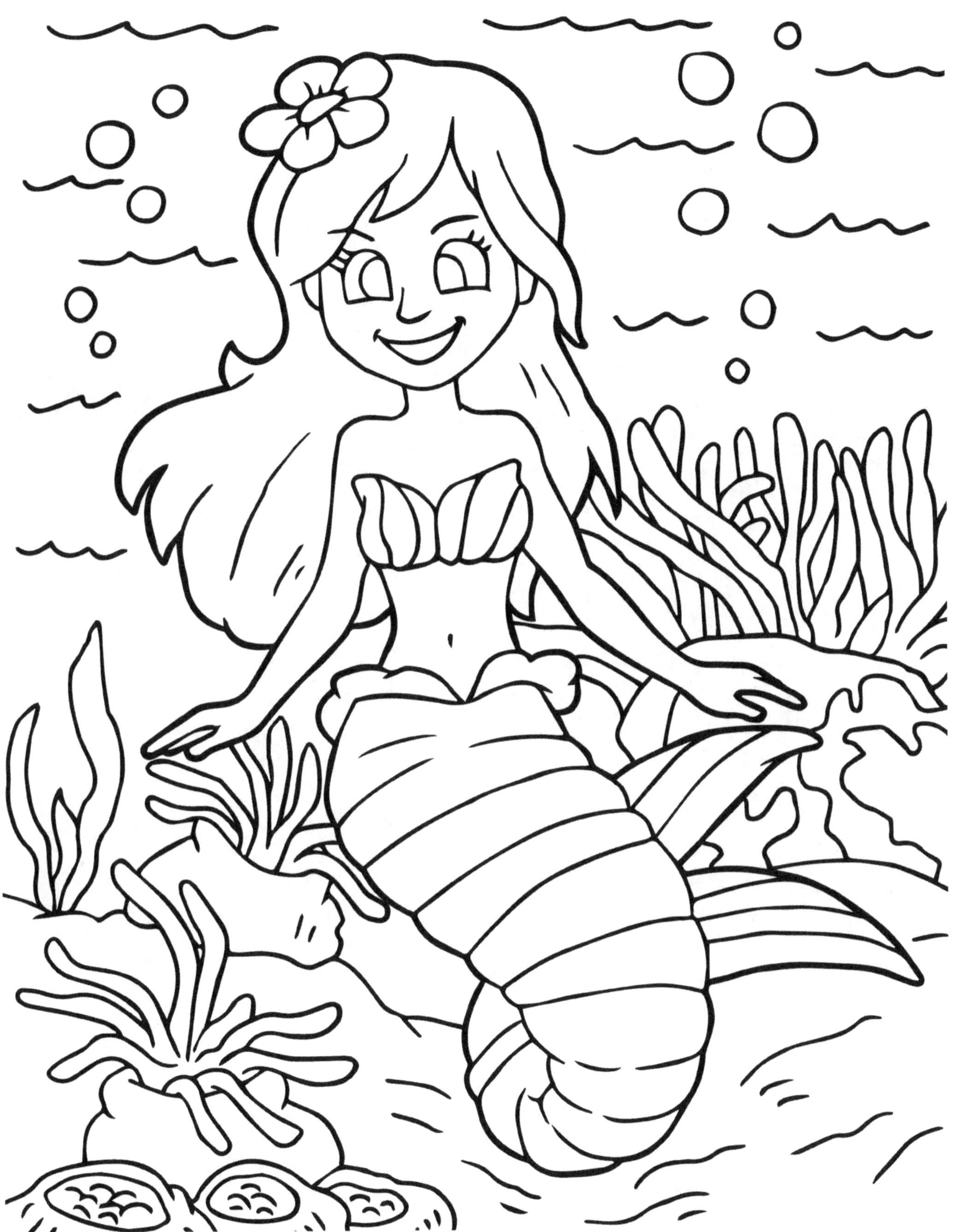

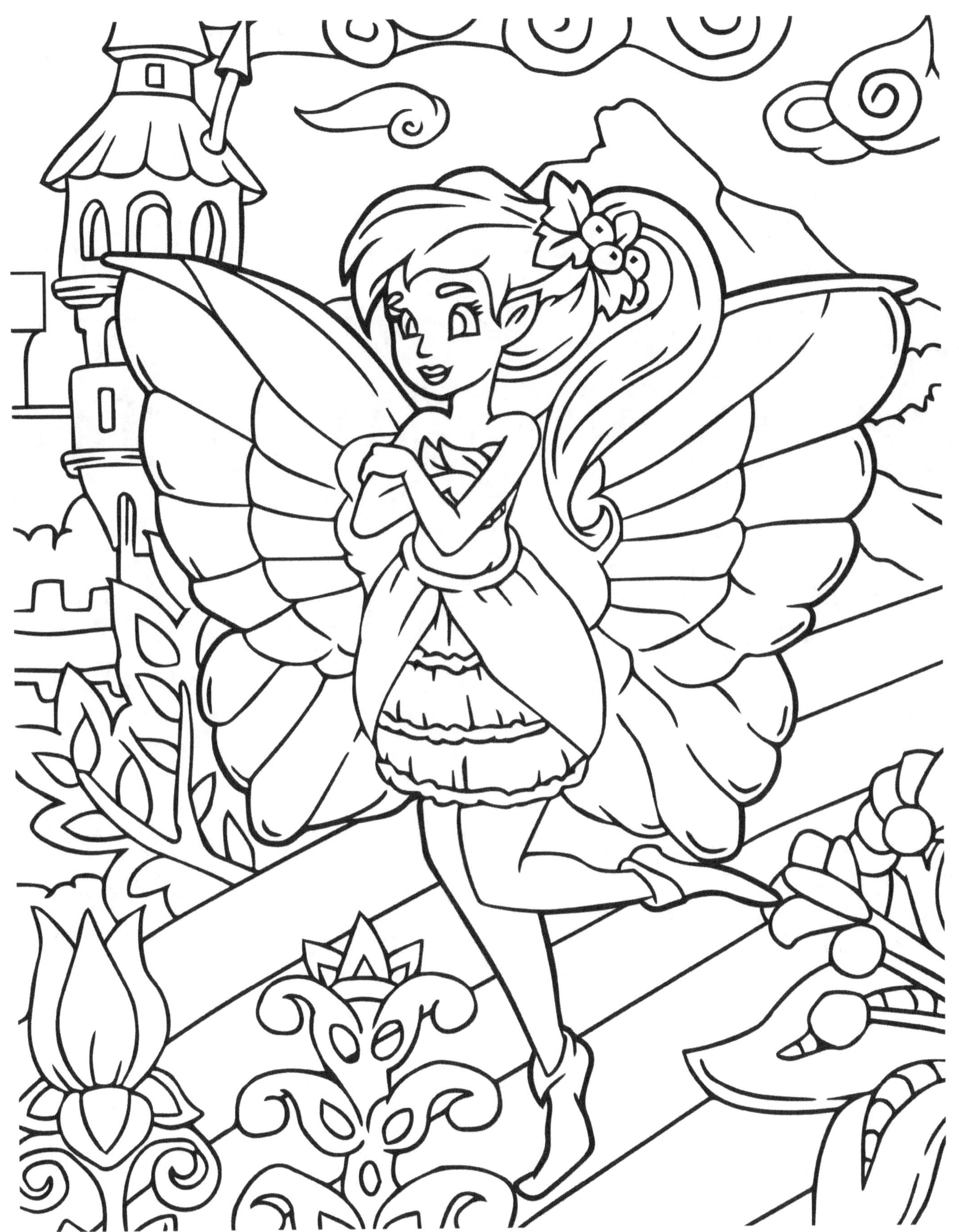

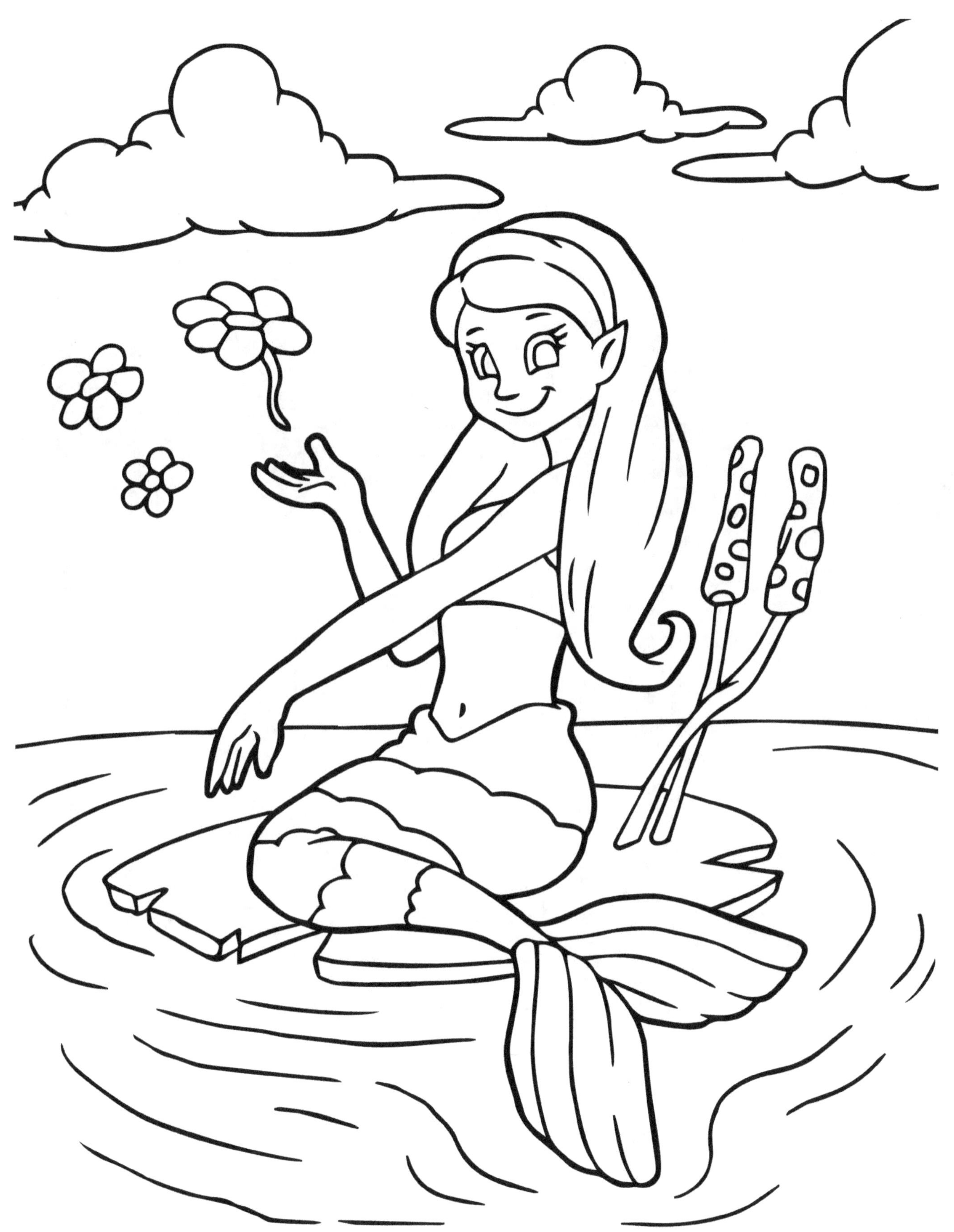

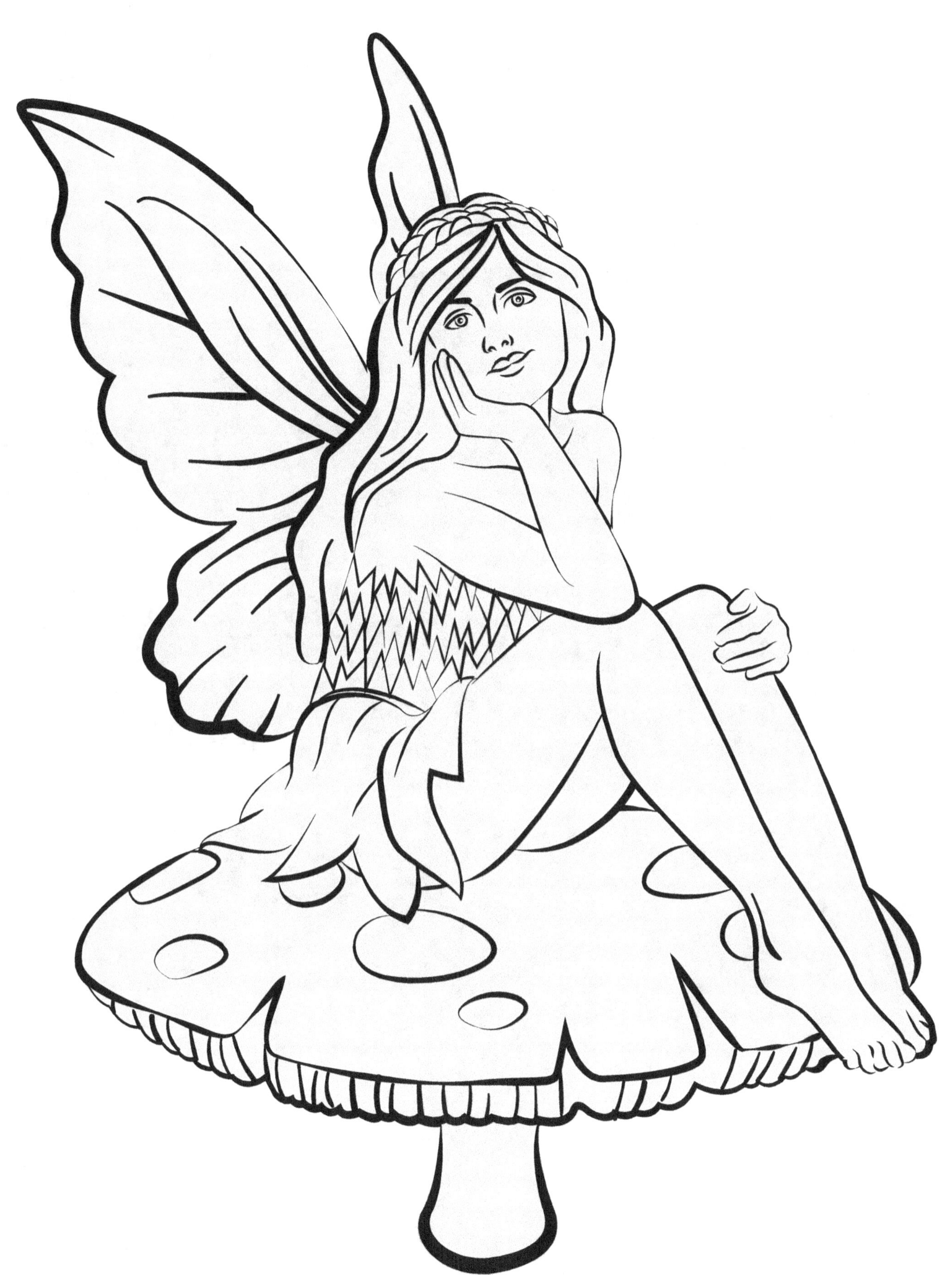

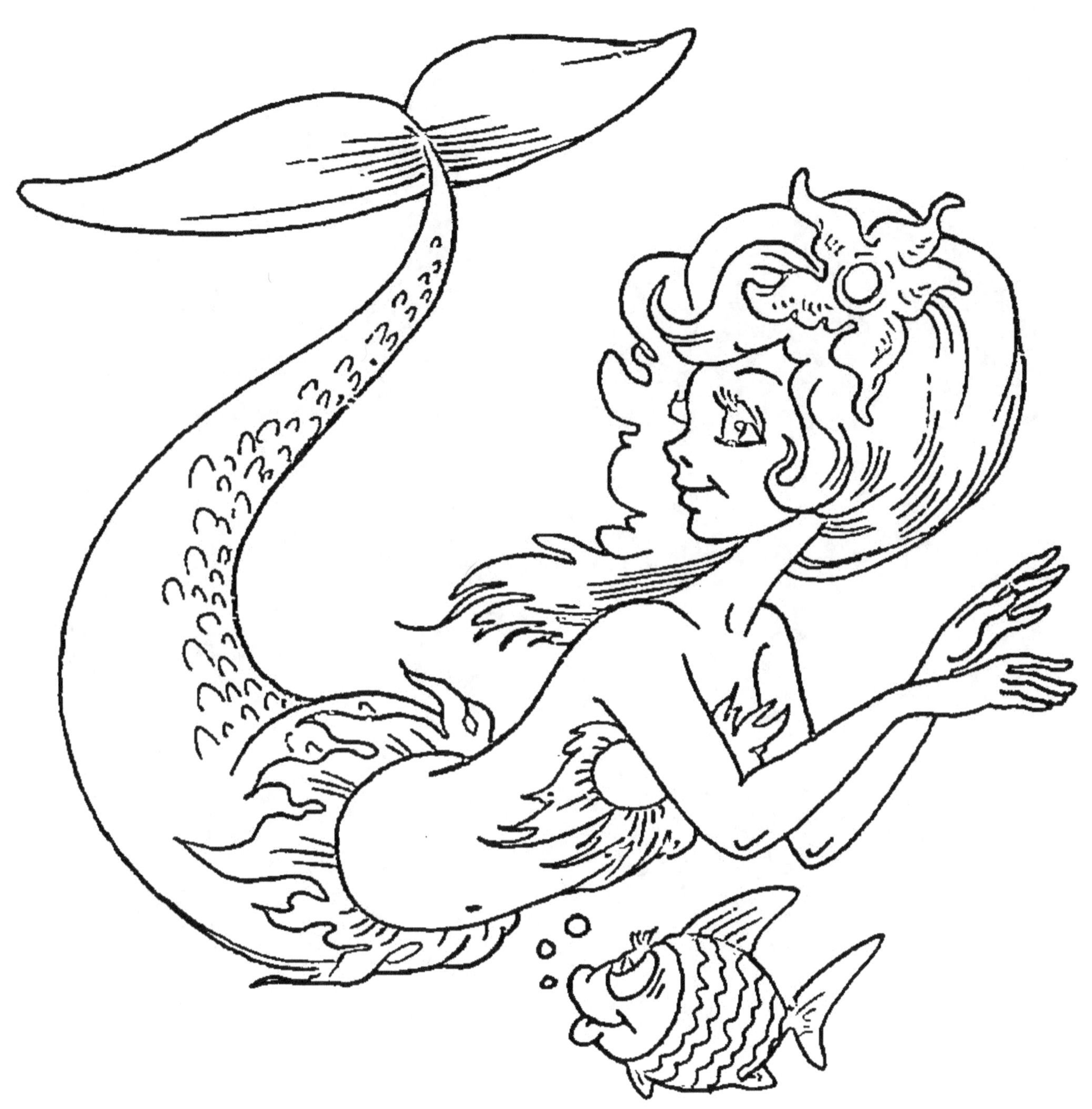

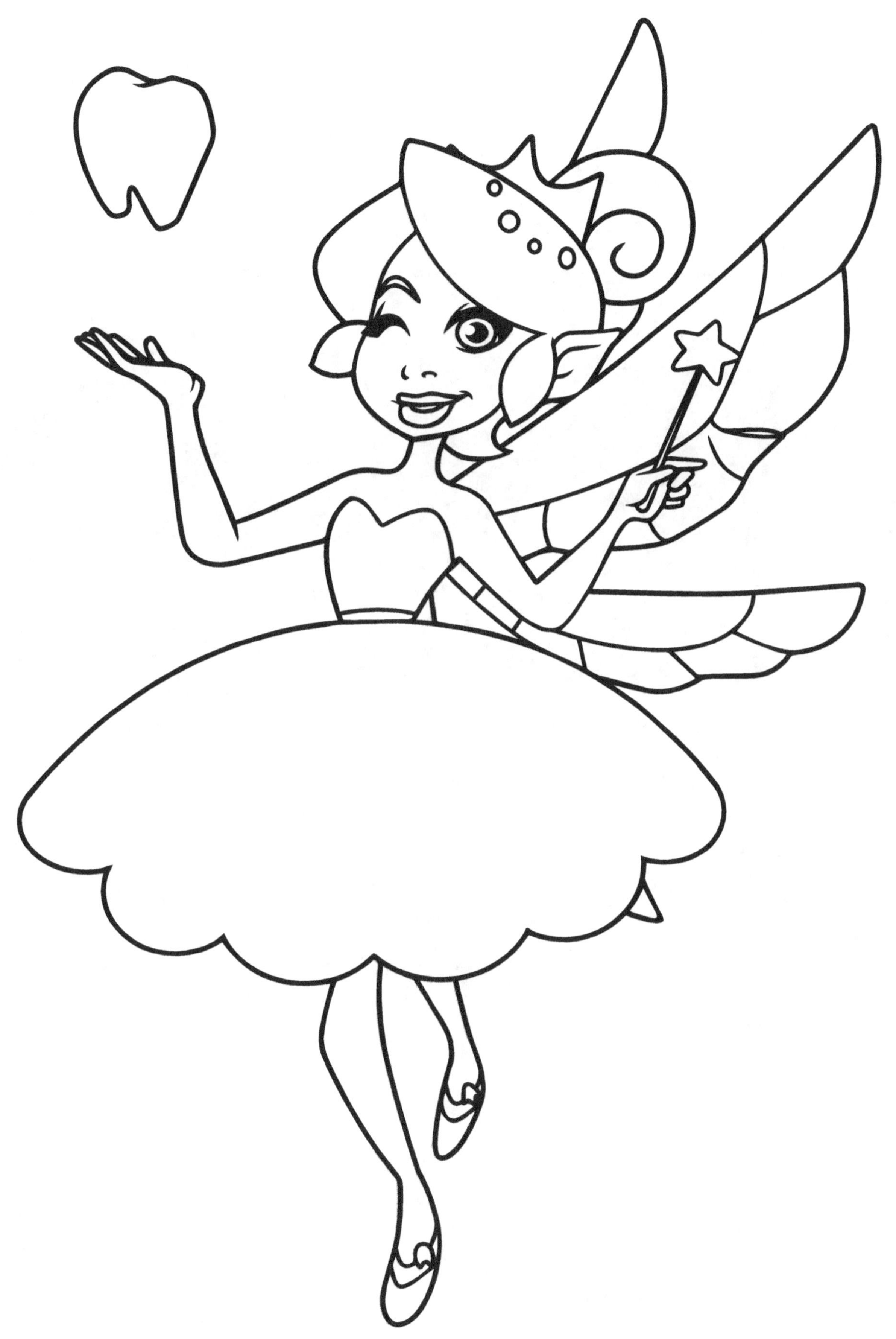

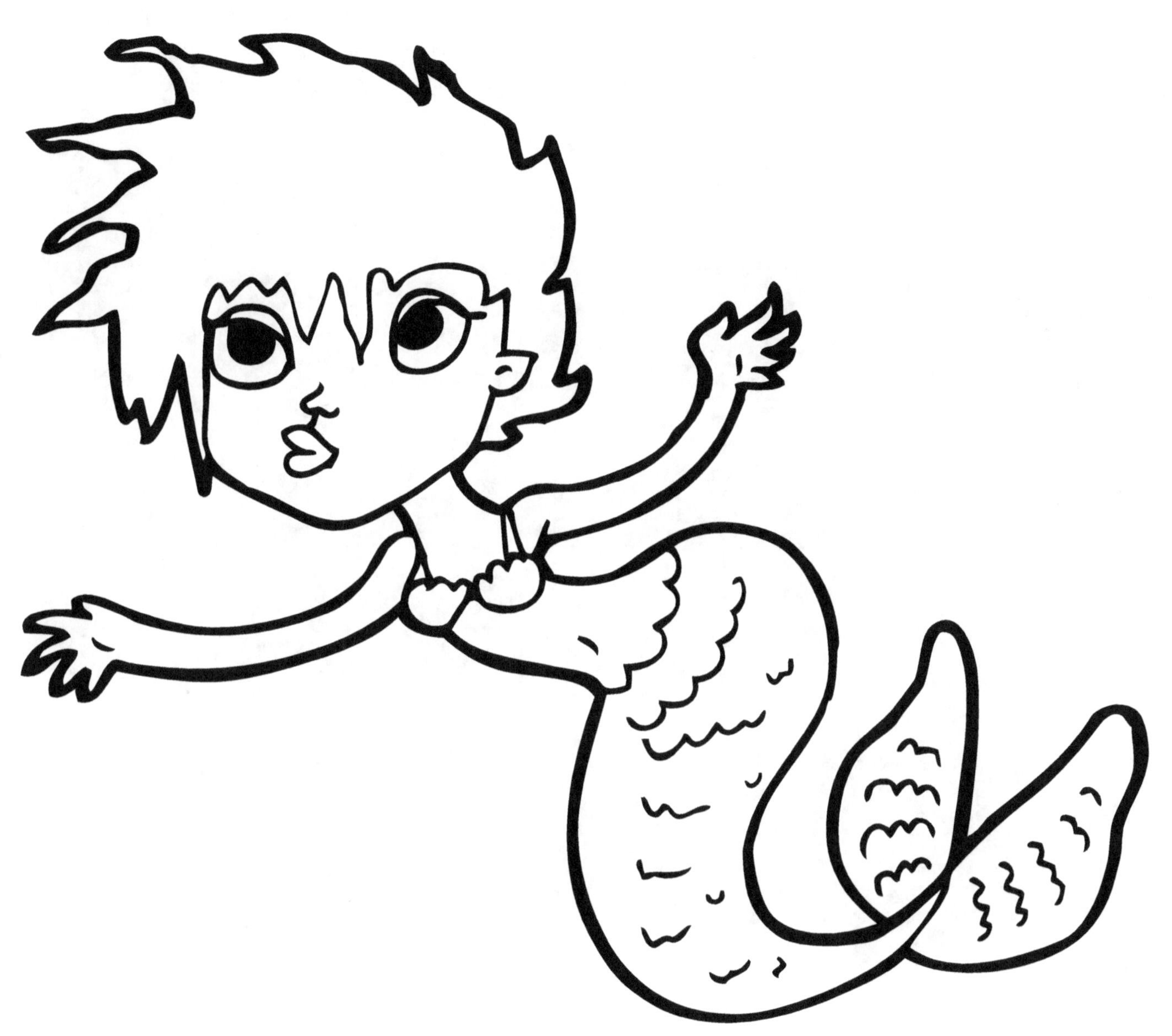